cooking
for friends

cooking
for friends

stylish recipes with great flavour

RYLAND
PETERS
& SMALL
LONDON NEW YORK

Alastair Hendy

photography by David Loftus

First published in the United States in 2000
by Ryland Peters & Small Inc.,
150 West 56th Street, Suite 6303
New York, NY 10019

10 9 8 7 6 5 4 3 2 1

Text © Alastair Hendy 1999 and 2000
Design and photographs
© Ryland Peters & Small 1999 and 2000

Printed and bound in China by Toppan Printing Co.

ISBN 1 84172 087 9

A CIP record for this book is available from the Library
of Congress.

Notes
All spoon measurements are level unless specified otherwise.
Ovens should be preheated to the specified temperature.
If using a fan-assisted oven, cooking times should be reduced
according to the manufacturer's instructions.
Specialist Asian ingredients are available in large supermarkets,
Thai, Chinese, Japanese and Vietnamese shops, as well as
Asian stores.

The material contained in this book was originally published in
four different titles: *Fresh from the Farmer's Market Spring; Fresh
from the Farmer's Market Summer; Fresh from the Farmer's
Market Fall;* and *Fresh from the Farmer's Market Winter*
(published in 1999).

Designer
Robin Rout
Design Assistant
Suzanne Coetzee
Editors
Elsa Petersen-Schepelern
Maddalena Bastianelli
Production
Patricia Harrington
Art Director
Gabriella Le Grazie
Publishing Directors
Anne Ryland
Alison Starling

*Stylist and
Food Stylist*
Alastair Hendy
Cooking Assistant
Kate Habershon
Photographer's Assistant
Tara Fisher

To a dedicated cook,
my sister, Catherine

contents

introduction 7

soups and appetizers 8

vegetables 34

fish and seafood 68

chicken and
other birds 92

meat 120

desserts 142

index 174

acknowledgments 176

Cooking is not just about the process of cooking. It's also about eating well, appreciating the ingredients and having a great time with friends. I can only be inspired to cook if I've got the right stuff to cook with: seasonal vegetables and fruit that are at their best, top-quality fresh fish and meat from animals that have roamed about a bit and have had a happy life.

Buying fruit and vegetables in season is the key to good cooking. Not only are they less expensive and more easily available, they taste of what they are. Their flavors have not been lost through being forced out of season or by refrigeration during transport. Fresh from their native soil, you get their true garden flavours in full force. Cooking them couldn't be simpler, as you need do little to them. Cooking now is about spontaneity; a freedom to cook without getting bogged down with fiddly procedures. A bundle of this and a handful of that is the way I like to cook. No mucking about in the kitchen with complicated sauces or fretting too much over weights and measures. A knife, a chopping board and a couple of pans is generally all you need. Flavors are fresh and should be kept that way, so cooking times are short. Creating food is also about care and love, and sometimes involves extra time and attention, such as creating a good stock or slow-cooking a beautiful ham.

Throughout each chapter I've suggested variations on the dishes: different ways of combining parts of recipes with other ingredients; these are there to spark your own ideas. If one of the ingredients in a recipe isn't available when you do the shopping, rather than hunt high and low for it—which face it, most of us haven't got time for—buy something else you see that catches your eye and try it out. Enjoy your ingredients.

This book is for everyone—cooks and noncooks, for those who are just starting out and for those who are looking for inspiration. If you're not an accomplished cook, just follow the recipes and all should be well. That's how I learnt to cook—from books. *Cooking for Friends* has short, quick recipes for when you want instant satisfaction as well as others that need time in the oven. It's for everyone who loves food and entertaining.

I like to think there are no rules when it comes to serving food. Traditionally it's been three courses—appetizer, entrée, and dessert—but nowadays, we tend not to worry too much with such formalities. After all, enjoying food is not about the order in which we eat it or how much we eat, it's more about what we eat. As long as what we eat tastes wonderful then that's what matters. One cooked course with some ripe cheese and a piece of fruit to follow can make a perfect meal. And without too much time spent fretting in the kitchen you'll be much more in the mood to enjoy it. My favorite way of eating is to sample a few different small courses—three small meze-like dishes to pick and nibble at—almost tapas style. When I'm eating out I find my fork strays into my friends' plates and, despite protestation from those who have chosen well, we usually all end up sharing everything. Eating is about sharing, enjoying good food with others, so why make it a course thing?

Appetizers can just as easily be turned into main courses. Often, too a first course could be all that you want but you need a little bit more of it. So just make more of it. Many of the recipes in this chapter can be treated as snacks or lunches, and the soups can easily be eaten as a meal in themselves with some warm crusty bread.

If you want to provide three courses, then a small bowl of soup to start is the answer. It can be made well in advance and you haven't got to fuss with it before serving. It's a simple option but if you want to make it more special, more of a meal, then add a few extra pre-prepared ingredients on serving: a bowl of thick pumpkin soup can be served with slices of goat cheese and roasted pumpkin seeds; a clear Asian broth can have noodles, cooked shellfish or chicken, and a smattering of fresh scented herbs strewn on top or a tomato and pepper soup can be served chilled with a spicy salsa. You can dress it up or keep it simple to fit your appetite or the occasion.

soups and appetizers

Asparagus soup with Asian greens

A clear, hot, and sour Asian-style soup that's light and refreshing. The asparagus is lightly blanched to retain it's nutrients and *al dente* crispness. Add rice noodles and cooked shrimp or chicken for a more substantial soup.

5 cups clear light chicken stock or 1 chicken stock cube dissolved in 5 cups hot water

1 tablespoon fish sauce*

3 teaspoons sugar

1 small hot chile, finely sliced

1 inch fresh ginger, finely sliced

2 stalks lemongrass, trimmed and smashed with a rolling pin

1 teaspoon tamarind paste*

1 bundle young asparagus tips, sprue, or wild asparagus

1 small bunch water spinach (*ong choi*), other Asian leaves, baby spinach leaves or watercress, trimmed of any tough stems*

4 scallions, chopped

juice of ½ lime

Crispy shallots (optional):

6 shallots, finely sliced

a pinch of salt

vegetable oil, for cooking

Serves 6

Note: Bottled fish sauce, tamarind paste, and other Asian ingredients such as water spinach and Chinese leaves are sold in Asian stores.

1

Put the stock, fish sauce, sugar, chile, ginger, lemongrass, and tamarind paste in a saucepan, bring to a boil, reduce the heat, and simmer for about 20 minutes.

2

Bring a large saucepan of salted water to a boil, plunge in the asparagus, return to a boil, simmer for 1 minute, then drain, rinse in cold water, and transfer to a bowl of ice water.

3

To make the crispy shallots, if using, put in a bowl and toss with salt. Heat the vegetable oil in a heavy-bottom skillet, add the shallots, and sauté until dark brown and crisp.

4

Divide the blanched asparagus, water spinach, and scallions between 6 small soup bowls. Reheat the stock if necessary, add the lime juice, then strain over the ingredients in the bowls, top with the crispy shallots, and serve.

Variations:

• Add other ingredients such as cooked shrimp, poached chicken, wide rice noodles, or tofu.

Chicken and butter leek soup

This is one of those antidote soups—cleansing, yet nourishing. Perfect for when you have overdone it and are hankering for something light but warm.

6 leeks

1 chicken, about 3lb., preferably free-range

2 carrots, halved

1 inch fresh ginger, peeled and thickly sliced

2 garlic cloves

2 teaspoons black peppercorns

1 fresh bouquet garni (3 fresh bay leaves tied together with large sprigs of parsley and tarragon)

¼ cup butter

1 tablespoon freshly squeezed lemon juice

a bunch of chives

sea salt and freshly ground black pepper

Serves 6

1

Slice 2 leeks in half lengthwise and rinse thoroughly under running water to remove all the dirt. Cut the remaining leeks into thick rounds, rinse well, and let soak in a bowl of cold water.

2

Put the chicken in a snug-fitting saucepan, add the halved leeks, carrots, ginger, garlic, peppercorns, and bouquet garni, and season generously. Cover with water, bring to a boil, skim off the froth, turn down the heat, cover, and simmer gently for 45 minutes.

3

Turn off the heat and let the chicken cool completely in the stock.

4

When cold, remove the bird from the pan, flake the meat from the bone and discard the skin and bones*. Strain the stock and reserve.

5

Put the sliced leeks in a single layer across a wide saucepan. Season, then add the butter and ½ cup of the stock. Heat to simmering, cover, and gently poach for about 5 minutes or until the leeks are tender. Reheat the strained stock with the flaked chicken meat, add the lemon juice, and spoon into bowls. Serve with the poached buttery leeks and a few chive stems.

__Note:__ If you want to make a richer stock, return the bones to the stock pot, cover, and simmer for 1 hour more, then strain and discard the bones.

Variation:

• Omit the ginger, add broken pieces of pasta to the strained soup stock, and cook as you reheat the chicken (a good way to use up all your dregs of pasta).

Pumpkin soup

with Creole roasted pumpkin seeds and goat cheese

A bowl of hot pumpkin soup on a cold wet fall day—add a slice or three of goat cheese and a good sprinkling of crisp pumpkin seeds and your soup will turn into a meal. Use dense-fleshed pumpkin with brown, gray, or dark green skins—orange-skinned varieties tend to be watery.

3 lb. pumpkin, halved and peeled

olive oil, for sautéing and baking

1 onion, finely chopped

2 garlic cloves, crushed

2 teaspoons cumin seeds, toasted

2 sprigs of thyme

2 bay leaves

½ teaspoon freshly grated nutmeg

1 teaspoon ground allspice

1½ quarts chicken stock

salt and freshly ground black pepper

1 goat cheese log or 1 small tub of goat curd cheese, to serve

Creole roasted pumpkin seeds:

2 teaspoons olive oil

½ teaspoon garlic salt

½ teaspoon onion powder

1 teaspoon paprika

a pinch of cayenne

1 teaspoon dried oregano

Serves 6

1

Remove and reserve the pumpkin seeds. Cut the pumpkin flesh into large chunks.

2

Heat 2 tablespoons olive oil in a deep skillet, add the onion and garlic, and sauté until soft. Add salt and pepper, the cumin seeds, thyme, bay leaves, nutmeg, and allspice. Sauté for 1 minute. Add the stock and pumpkin and simmer gently for about 30 minutes or until soft. Purée in a food processor, transfer to a saucepan, and keep it warm.

3

Clean the fibers off the pumpkin seeds, then toss the seeds with the olive oil, garlic salt, onion powder, paprika, cayenne, and oregano. Spread over a baking tray and roast in a preheated oven at 400°F for 10–15 minutes.

4

Serve the soup accompanied by the toasted seeds and slices of goat cheese.

Variations:

• Replace the toasted pumpkin seeds with fried crispy sage leaves.

• Use freshly grated Parmesan or Gruyère instead of goat cheese.

Tomato and pepper soup

with eggplant croutons

It's important to use good, well-flavored tomatoes for this soup—use Italian plum or the so called "vine-ripened" varieties. Water is used instead of stock, to keep the flavors clean and sharp—perfect for the strict nonmeat eaters.

6 large red bell peppers, preferably the long, tapered Italian variety

6 tablespoons olive oil

1 large onion, chopped

2 garlic cloves, halved

3 lb. tomatoes, chopped

leaves and stalks from 8 sprigs of cilantro (preferably with roots) or basil

a pinch of sugar

1 teaspoon Tabasco (optional)

1 eggplant, quartered lengthwise, inner flesh discarded, flesh cut into small cubes

sea salt and freshly ground black pepper

Serves 6

1

Put the bell peppers directly on the gas flame of your stovetop. Turn every minute or so until blackened and blistered all over. Alternatively, roast in a preheated oven at 425°F for about 20 minutes. Put them in a covered bowl and let cool. Scrape off the charred peel, then core, and seed the flesh.

2

Heat 2 tablespoons olive oil in a skillet, add the onion and garlic, and sauté until softened and transparent. Add the peppers, tomatoes, herb stalks, sugar, salt, and pepper. Stew gently for 20 minutes, add 2¾ cups water, and stew for a further 20 minutes.

3

Sieve the mixture into a clean saucepan, pushing through all the flesh, and discarding the skins and seeds. Add the Tabasco, if using, warm through (but don't boil), then serve.

4

Season the eggplant, then heat the remaining oil in the skillet. Add the eggplant and sauté until golden. Add to the bowls of soup and top with cilantro or basil leaves.

Variations:

• Add chopped black olives and basil or avocado, or sautéed zucchini, or even fried calamari, or feta cheese at the same time as the eggplant.

• Omit the peppers from the recipe and serve the soup chilled with a Bloody Mary salsa (chopped avocado, tomatoes, and cilantro, with grated red onion, lime juice, and vodka).

Jerusalem artichoke chowder
with pan-seared scallops

Chowder (a thick white seafood soup flavored with bacon) is traditionally thickened with potato. Using Jerusalem artichokes gives it a wintry earthiness, and the scallops elevate the humble soup to restaurant status. Jerusalem artichokes are not artichokes, but tubers like potatoes. These knobbly and earthy vegetables have a pronounced sweet flavor.

8 large scallops

2 tablespoons olive oil

1 lb. Jerusalem artichokes

2 tablespoons butter

1 leek, white part only, rinsed and finely chopped

1 bay leaf

2 sprigs of thyme

3 potatoes, diced

3 slices bacon

1 cup crème fraîche or sour cream

1¼ cups milk

1¾ cups chicken stock

a squeeze of fresh lemon juice

sea salt and freshly ground black pepper

Serves 8 as an appetizer, 4 for supper

1

Trim the scallops if necessary and slice in half to make 16 rounds. Season, toss in the olive oil, and set aside.

2

Peel and dice the Jerusalem artichokes and, as you do so, put them into a bowl of water acidulated with a dash of lemon juice to prevent discoloration.

3

Heat the butter in a saucepan, add the leek, bay leaf, and thyme and sauté until soft. Add the Jerusalem artichokes and potatoes, and cook for 1 minute more. Add the bacon, crème fraîche, milk, stock, lemon juice, and seasoning. Bring to a boil, reduce the heat, and simmer for 20 minutes or until soft.

4

Discard the bay leaf and bacon and, using a food processor or hand blender (which will give you a "cappuccino" froth), blend to a smooth purée. Add extra stock or milk if it needs thinning, then taste and adjust the seasoning.

5

Heat a heavy-bottom skillet until smoking hot and sear the scallops for 30 seconds on each side. Put the hot soup into bowls and add slices of seared scallop to each one.

Variation:

• Use freshly steamed cockles instead of scallops. Add them and their juices to the soup.

Spice island noodle soup

with dumplings

The spice islands of Indonesia still retain their plantations of nutmeg, clove, cinnamon, and nuts. I dreamt up this recipe while sitting on top of an island volcano, looking over the spice groves below. It contains all these wonderful spice and nut flavors—trapped in a delicious dumpling.

1¼ quarts light chicken stock

2 stalks lemongrass, trimmed and smashed

8 kaffir lime leaves, torn,
or the juice of ½ lime, plus 1 teaspoon sugar

2 garlic cloves, thickly sliced

1½ inches fresh ginger, thickly sliced

1 package rice vermicelli noodles, about 1 oz., soaked in hot water for 4 minutes, drained, and rinsed

Chinese leaves, such as bok choy

Spice dumplings:

8 oz. peeled shrimp, fresh or frozen and thawed

8 oz. ground pork

1½ inches fresh ginger, peeled and finely grated

2 tablespoons finely chopped cilantro

2½ oz. canned bamboo shoots, drained

16 macadamia nuts

4 scallions, trimmed and chopped

2 small red chiles, finely chopped

½ tablespoon *kecap manis* or dark soy sauce

1 tablespoon fish sauce or 1 teaspoon salt

2 tablespoons lime juice

a pinch of ground cloves

a pinch of ground cinnamon

1 small egg, lightly beaten, to bind

vegetable oil, for sautéing

Serves 6

1

Put the chicken stock, lemongrass, lime leaves or juice, and sugar, garlic, and ginger in a saucepan, bring to a boil and simmer, covered, for about 20 minutes. Taste and add salt if necessary. Strain into a clean pan and discard the flavorings.

2

To make the dumplings, put the shrimp in a food processor and chop for 1–2 seconds. Transfer to a bowl. Add all the remaining ingredients except the egg and oil to the processor and work to a coarse crumb consistency. Mix with the shrimp and egg. Roll the mixture into walnut-sized balls and chill for 30 minutes.

3

Heat the oil in a skillet or deep-fryer, add the dumplings in batches and cook gently until golden brown all over, about 2–3 minutes. Remove and set aside.

4

To serve, reheat the broth and arrange a share of noodles and a few leaves in 6 deep soup bowls. Divide the dumplings between the bowls and pour over the hot lime broth.

Variations:

• Use Brazil nuts instead of macadamia nuts.

• Spear each dumpling with a bamboo skewer, sauté, and serve with drinks.

Asparagus brunch with prosciutto toasts

The traditional way to cook asparagus is to stand the bundle upright in a tall saucepan and simmer in a few inches of water. However, you will need a special pan; instead, simmer the spears in salted water for a few minutes in an ordinary pan, or steam in a metal or bamboo steamer.

6 large eggs

1 bundle green asparagus (about 30 spears)

sea salt and cracked black pepper

butter, for brushing

Prosciutto toast:

6–12 slices white or brown bread, toasted

butter, for spreading

6–12 slices finely cut prosciutto

Serves 6

1

To cook soft-boiled eggs, prick the blunt ends to prevent cracking, put into a saucepan of cold water and bring to a boil. When the water reaches boiling point, set the timer for 4 minutes for soft eggs, 5 for harder yolks. Put into egg cups set on 6 dinner plates.

2

To prepare the asparagus, steam for a few minutes (or simmer in salted water) until tender but still crisp—test with the point of a knife. Remove from the steamer, brush with melted butter, and divide between the dinner plates.

3

Toast the bread, spread with butter, trim the crusts, and cut into 2–3 lengths. Wrap with prosciutto and add to the plates. Serve with sea salt and freshly cracked black pepper.

4

To eat, dip the proscuitto toasts and the asparagus tips into the egg.

Roasted tomatoes in herb oil

with char-grilled bread and baby mozzarella

I love it when restaurants give you a saucer of olive oil and balsamic vinegar plus bread and a few olives—just to keep your stomach occupied while you make a decision over the menu. It looks good, needs virtually no preparation, and tastes great—so why not do it at home. Keep it as simple as that, or add sliced tomato and a few basil leaves, or do a little extra preparation, and try this idea—dishes to dip into or pile on to grilled bread—a self-assembly toast. This barely needs a recipe.

12 small to medium tomatoes

2–4 tablespoons chopped herbs, such as basil, dill, parsley, oregano, marjoram, and/or chives

2 tablespoons extra virgin olive oil

1 or 2 ciabatta loaves, sliced

1 fat garlic clove, halved

1 teaspoon balsamic vinegar

6 baby fresh mozzarella or 1 large mozzarella, cut into chunks

sea salt flakes and coarsely crushed black pepper

Serves 6

1

Roast the tomatoes in a preheated oven at 425°F for about 8 minutes. Cool, peel, and put in a bowl.

2

Mix the herbs with the oil, pour over the tomatoes and let stand for a few hours or overnight.

3

When ready to serve, char-grill the slices of bread on both sides, then rub with the cut garlic clove. Put the sea salt and pepper in separate small dishes.

4

Drain the tomatoes and reserve the oil. Put the tomatoes in a small dish and strain the oil into another, adding a splash of balsamic vinegar. Add a small dish of the mozzarella.

5

Make up your own toast at the table, or eat the tomato and mozzarella separately and dip the toast in the balsamic oil.

Variations:

• Add extra dishes, such as jars of vegetable antipasto and cured meats from a gourmet store.

• Serve other dishes such as salami, prosciutto, oven-roasted tomatoes (page 80), roasted vine tomatoes and bean salad (page 38) or char-grilled eggplant (page 126).

Green fruit gado gado
with lime and peanut dressing

Classic Indonesian gado gado is a salad of blanched shredded vegetables, cucumber, and hard-cooked eggs with a sweet, hot, peanut dressing. Unripe (known as green) papaya and mango are common to Asian salads—they're best when finely shredded and tenderized with heavily lime-juiced dressings.

⅔ cup skinned unsalted peanuts, coarsely crushed

1 garlic clove

½ teaspoon salt

2 small red chiles, seeded and chopped

6 tablespoons brown sugar or palm sugar

4 limes

½ tablespoon sugar

selection of sour fruits, such as green (unripe) mango, green (unripe) papaya, starfruit or cucumber, peeled, pitted or seeded, and shredded* as necessary

a handful of basil, cilantro, and mint leaves

Serves 6 as an appetizer

Note: A mandoline is the best tool for shredding the fruits or cucumbers.

1
Dry-roast the crushed peanuts in a hot skillet until toasted and flecked with brown all over.

2
Using a mortar and pestle, pound the garlic and salt until puréed. Add the chiles and pound until mashed. Pound in the brown sugar, then the toasted peanuts (if your mortar is full, do in batches). Don't grind all the peanuts to fine granules: some should remain coarsely crushed. Stir in the juice of 2 limes (use a little juice earlier if the mixture is too stiff to work).

3
Mix the sugar with the juice of 1 lime until dissolved. Toss the prepared fruits and herbs in the sweetened lime juice.

4
Cut the skin and pith from the remaining lime and slice out the segments from the surrounding membrane.

5
To assemble the salad, put small mounds of the sour fruit and herb salad on each dish (I use a 2-pronged carving fork to twist the salad like spaghetti). Top with the chile peanut dressing and cover loosely with more salad and lime segments.

Variations:

- Eat the salad and peanut dressing wrapped up in lettuce leaves.
- Add freshly grated or shavings of coconut.
- Serve on banana petals with chopsticks—purple banana flowers are available from specialist Asian food stores.

Avocado and cilantro toast

Avocado has to be the perfect food—convenient, delicious, and good for you. The dark, warty-skinned Haas variety has the best flavor and texture. It goes well with many herbs, but cilantro is especially good.

2 ripe avocados, halved and pitted

juice of 1 lime, plus extra, for sprinkling

2 tablespoons virgin olive oil, plus extra for sprinkling

green jalapeño Tabasco sauce (or regular), to taste

4–8 slices bread, such as cornmeal, ciabatta, or crusty farmhouse white

a bunch of cilantro sprigs, thoroughly washed and drained, stems removed

sea salt and freshly cracked black pepper

Serves 4–6

Variations:

Pile higher with:

• Cooked shrimp or crab marinated in sweetened lime juice.

• Poached chicken and toasted cumin seeds.

• Orange-scented olive oil, chopped spring onion, and cherry tomatoes.

1

Using a fork, mash the avocado flesh with the lime juice, 2 tablespoons of the olive oil, the Tabasco, salt and pepper.

2

Char-grill or toast the bread on both sides and sprinkle with a little salt and extra oil.

3

Spread the avocado thickly over the toast, sprinkle with the remaining olive oil and lime juice, salt, and pepper. Pile cilantro on top.

Roasted mushrooms

with horseradish mascarpone

Mushrooms on toast are, for me, the definitive mushroom meal. Simple and straight to the point. Though I don't usually like to muck about with it, this recipe with hot horseradish and thyme still follows the purist path—the combination is wonderful.

6 large open mushrooms, stems removed, caps well brushed

a bunch of thyme

½ cup butter, softened, plus extra, for greasing

3 garlic cloves, crushed

6 thick slices white bread, toasted

sea salt and freshly ground black pepper

Horseradish mascarpone:

2 inches fresh horseradish root, peeled and grated, or 2 tablespoons horseradish sauce

1 cup mascarpone cheese

Serves 6

1

Thoroughly mix the horseradish and mascarpone and set aside.

2

Put the mushrooms, gills upward, in a greased roasting pan. Sprinkle with sea salt and pepper, and tuck the thyme around them.

3

Mix two-thirds of the butter with the garlic and dot over the mushrooms. Roast in a preheated oven at 375°F for about 10 minutes.

4

Spread the toast with the remaining butter. Add a mushroom and a spoonful of the horseradish mascarpone to each slice. Sprinkle with the thyme leaves and serve.

Pea quiche

Classic quiche, with eggs, cream, and salty bacon. You can't beat it! Add fresh cooked peas and nothing could be easier, or taste and look so good— one course in a slice. Serve plain, or top with more peas and a sprig of basil.

1 package frozen shortcrust pastry, about 1 lb., thawed

1 tablespoon olive oil

3 oz. pancetta or bacon lardons

1 garlic clove, finely chopped

2½ cups cooked green peas

1 tablespoon torn fresh tarragon or basil

4 eggs, beaten (retain a spoonful for brushing the pastry)

¾ cup double cream

sea salt and freshly ground black pepper

To serve (optional):

about 1 cup shelled peas, cooked

sprigs of basil or mint

Serves 4–6

1

Roll out the pastry and use to line the base and sides of a deep 6-inch springform or loose-bottom cake pan. Prick the base of the pastry and chill.

2

Heat the oil in a skillet, add the pancetta or bacon, sauté until crisp, then stir in the garlic. Sprinkle the crispy mixture over the base of the pastry, fill the case with peas, then sprinkle with tarragon or basil.

3

Put the eggs, cream, salt, and pepper in a bowl, beat well, then pour the mixture into the pie shell. Brush the pastry with the reserved egg and cover loosely with foil.

4

Bake in a preheated oven at 400°F for about 45 minutes or until set. Check after 20 minutes: if the top is browning, cover the top of the quiche with foil and move to the bottom shelf of the oven. Serve warm as is, or topped with a pile of peas and sprigs of basil or mint.

Variations:

• Use ¾ cup ricotta instead of cream, and add layers of blanched sliced zucchini.

Gone are the days when vegetables were just "two vegetables" that sat alongside the meat, and gone too are the days when vegetables on their own, without meat, were for vegetarians only. With the globalization of our cooking and availability of world produce, we can now do so much more with our vegetables. I live on vegetables. Not because they're good for me but because I like eating them, they have such breadth and depth of flavor. I eat meat and fish too, but I wouldn't notice or feel I'd missed out somewhere if I'd had neither in a week.

For vegetables to be good, they must be fresh. That may sound a bit obvious, but so often we make do with what we are offered. Supermarket neatly packaged salad and perfectly boxed red tomatoes may look the part but how fresh are they? And what about flavor? If they are not in season then the chances are they've come a long way, from another part of the globe. They will not be as fresh as home grown and will lack the flavors we look for. Try and stick to vegetables that are in season and if you're not sure what comes when, here are a few pointers: they will be piled high because they're plentiful; they will look vibrant because they're brand spanking fresh; and should be about half the price they normally are because they're home grown. And that too explains why you should want them in the first place. They are the best. When I cook with vegetables, I like to try and keep them looking and tasting of what they are, only enhanced by what is added. The perfect food can be as simple as a plate of sun-warmed sliced tomatoes annointed with good virgin oil; a dish of freshly pulled and boiled buttered root vegetables; or a bowl of creamy mashed potatoes fragrant with saffron butter. All good enough to eat on their own. Take pleasure in the best. Look forward to, anticipate and relish the roots, stems, and greens of the season—it makes cooking easy.

vegetables

Caesar greens
with anchovy baked toast

Use tender open-hearted greens or Italian cavolo nero (black cabbage)—a fine sweet cabbage that needs only the simplest of cooking. It is very good with anchovies and with this creamy Parmesan dressing and salty anchovy baked toasts. "Eat up your greens"—happily.

mixed open-heart winter greens, cavolo nero if possible, trimmed and tough stems removed

⅔ cup fresh, finely grated Parmesan cheese

Anchovy baked toast:

butter, for spreading

1 baguette, thinly sliced diagonally

1 can anchovy fillets puréed with a dash of Worcestershire sauce

Creamy dressing:

2 egg yolks

1 garlic clove, crushed

2 tablespoons sherry vinegar

¾ cup olive oil

2 tablespoons light cream

sea salt and freshly ground black pepper

Serves 6

Variations:

• Finely slice the greens and toss into cooked pasta with the dressing, the Parmesan, and finely chopped anchovy fillets.

• Dip veal escalopes in seasoned flour, then in beaten egg, then in breadcrumbs. Sauté in butter on both sides. Add 4 finely chopped canned anchovies to the dressing. Serve the schnitzel with the Caesar greens.

1

For the dressing; beat the egg yolks in a bowl with the garlic, vinegar, and seasoning. Beat in the olive oil thoroughly, then the cream.

2

To make the toasts, butter the baguette slices, arrange on a baking tray, and cook in a preheated oven at 375°F until crisp. Spread thinly with the anchovy mixture.

3

Blanch the greens in boiling salted water for about 1 minute (tougher greens will need 5 minutes). Drain and toss with the dressing and sprinkle heavily with the Parmesan. Serve the greens piled onto the anchovy toasts.

Roasted vine tomatoes

with cannellini bean salad and tapenade oil

Tomatoes grow on bushes, not vines, yet we call tomatoes sold on the stem "vine tomatoes," probably because they look vaguely like a bunch of grapes. Roasted on their stems, they keep that just-picked look on the plate.

6 "vines" of baby tomatoes, about 6 fruit each

extra virgin olive oil, for brushing and dressing

2 cans cannellini beans, about 14 oz. each, rinsed and drained

1 medium red onion, finely chopped

2 garlic cloves, crushed

3 tablespoons coarsely chopped flat-leaf parsley or torn basil leaves

2 tablespoons ready-made tapenade*

½ teaspoon sugar

juice of 1 lemon

sea salt and cracked black pepper

Serves 6

*Tapanade, or olive paste, is available in Italian gourmet stores and larger supermarkets.

1

Arrange the tomato "vines" in a single layer on a baking tray, brush with olive oil, and sprinkle with salt and pepper. Roast in a preheated oven at about 425°F for 6–8 minutes, until the peel has lightly blistered.

2

Put the beans, onion, garlic, parsley, and tapenade in a bowl and stir gently. Dissolve the sugar in the lemon juice and add to the bean mixture. Stir in about 2 tablespoons olive oil and let stand at room temperature for 30 minutes.

3

To serve, spread the bean salad over serving plates, add a "vine" of tomatoes to each plate, spoon over any remaining bean dressing and tomato roasting juices, and dress liberally with more olive oil.

Variations:

• Make into a more substantial course by adding flakes of blackened salmon (page 80), roasted cod, sautéed mullet, or barbecued monkfish kebobs.

• Give it the niçoise treatment and mix the tapenade with mayonnaise, add halved hard-cooked eggs, anchovies, and rare-roasted tuna.

Fava bean falafels with herb radish salad

Falafels are the pride of Lebanese cooking, starring favorite Middle Eastern herbs like mint, parsley, and cilantro. Don't be discouraged by the long list of ingredients—this recipe is very simple.

1 cup shelled fava beans

1 cup chickpeas (garbanzo beans), soaked overnight in cold water to cover

3 garlic cloves, crushed

4 scallions, chopped

1 heaped tablespoon chopped parsley

1 heaped tablespoon chopped cilantro

1 heaped tablespoon chopped dill

1 heaped tablespoon chopped mint

3 teaspoons ground coriander

3 teaspoons ground cumin and 1 teaspoon cumin seeds, pan-toasted

3–4 tablespoons olive oil

1 tablespoon lemon juice

1 teaspoon baking powder mixed with 2 tablespoons warm water

4 tablespoons sesame seeds, half pan-toasted, half plain

sea salt and freshly ground black pepper

6 warmed pitta breads, to serve (optional)

vegetable oil, for frying

1

Put the fava beans, chickpeas, garlic, scallions, herbs, cumin, olive oil, lemon juice, and baking powder mixture in a food processor and process to a coarse paste. Add salt and pepper to taste. Chill.

2

Roll the falafel mixture into walnut-sized balls. Roll one third of the balls in the plain sesame seeds and another third in the toasted sesame seeds. Leave the remainder plain. Heat the oil in a skillet, saucepan, or wok and gently sauté or deep-fry the falafels until golden. Drain on crumpled paper towels.

3

To make the salad, put the yogurt, lemon juice, tahini paste, salt, and pepper in a bowl and beat with a fork. Add the salad leaves, herbs, cucumber, and radish. Toss gently.

4

Serve the falafels with the salad on plates or in warm pitta bread.

Herb radish salad:

4 tablespoons plain yogurt

1 teaspoon lemon juice

1 teaspoon tahini paste

assorted salad leaves and herbs, such as mizuna, golden orach, misome, mint, and cilantro

3 inches cucumber, finely sliced

6 radishes, finely sliced

sea salt and freshly ground black pepper

Serves 6

41

Tomato and bell pepper tart

Use red bell peppers with red cherry tomatoes and yellow peppers with yellow cherry tomatoes. If you prefer, you can also make this tart with tomatoes only (buy 2 baskets extra). Yogurt cheese needs a bit of planning and a square of cheesecloth (this quantity of yogurt makes more than you'll need for this tart—use the rest on toast or with cheese crackers. If you don't have time to make your own cheese, use soft cream cheese instead.

2 cups plain yogurt

1 teaspoon salt

1 large garlic clove, crushed

3 tablespoons finely chopped mixed fresh herbs, such as parsley, basil, chives, dill, and tarragon, plus sprigs for serving

½ package frozen puff pastry, 8 oz., thawed

1 basket cherry tomatoes, about 20

3 canned red bell peppers or pimientos, drained, seeded, and sliced lengthwise

1 egg, lightly beaten, to glaze

Serves 6

Variations:

• Spread the pastry with a layer of tapenade and top with tomatoes.

• Cover with sliced tomatoes, bake, and serve with fresh pesto.

• Flavor the yogurt cheese with toasted cumin seeds, sprinkle with paprika, and eat with toast.

1

Two days in advance, mix the yogurt, salt, and garlic in a small bowl or pitcher. Place a large square of cheesecloth into a large bowl and pour in the yogurt mixture. Gather up the corners and sides and tie tightly with string. Tie the bundle to a long-handled spoon and suspend over a deep container. Chill for 2 days to allow the whey to drain from the yogurt.

2

When ready to cook, discard the whey, put the yogurt cheese into a bowl and mix in the chopped herbs.

3

Roll out the pastry to a rectangle or circle and spread with half the cheese, leaving a ½-inch border around the edges. Top with the whole baby tomatoes and strips of peppers or pimiento. Brush the edges of the pastry with beaten egg.

4

Bake in a preheated oven at 425°F for 35 minutes or until the pastry has risen and is golden. Sprinkle with herb sprigs and serve hot

Asparagus phyllo tart with spinach

Asparagus might have been specially made for the tart treatment—use long spears for a square pan or short ones for a rectangular pan.

1 bundle asparagus, about 15 long spears or 20 short, ends trimmed

1 bunch spinach, about 20 large leaves, washed and trimmed

2 large potatoes, sliced

¼ cup butter, melted (reserve a tablespoon for glazing the pastry)

1 lb. phyllo pastry

1¾ cups Gruyère, grated

½ teaspoon freshly grated nutmeg

3 eggs, lightly beaten

1 cup heavy cream

sea salt and freshly ground black pepper

olive oil, for poaching

To serve:

4 oz. Parmesan cheese, in the piece, shaved with a vegetable peeler

a small handful of chives

Serves 4

1

Plunge the asparagus into a pan of boiling water, remove immediately, drain, and refresh in ice water. Drain. Pat dry with paper towels. Do the same with the spinach.

2

Put the potato slices in a saucepan, cover with olive oil, heat gently, then poach without browning until tender. Remove, then strain and reserve the oil for another use.

3

Brush a 9-inch square pie pan or 14 x 4 inch rectangular pan with a little melted butter and line with a sheet of phyllo pastry. Brush with more butter and top with another sheet of phyllo. Repeat until all the sheets are used. Trim the edges.

4

To assemble the tart, arrange a layer of cooked potato in the bottom of the pastry-lined pan. Season lightly with salt, pepper, and nutmeg. Add a layer of spinach and season again. Add the Gruyère and a second layer of potatoes and spinach, seasoning each one.

5

Beat the eggs and cream in a pitcher or bowl, then pour over the potatoes and spinach. Arrange a line of cooked asparagus over the top of the tart. Brush the pastry with the reserved butter.

6

Bake in a preheated oven at 350°F for 30–35 minutes. Halfway through cooking, cover the asparagus, but not the pastry edge, with foil or buttered parchment paper. When the center of the tart is just set, remove it from the oven and serve with Parmesan curls and chives.

Summer pasta

This isn't a regular baked lasagne: it's much lighter, like a dressed summer pasta—a light and fruity tomato salsa with zucchini and basil, under a blanket of ricotta and pasta.

6 sprigs of basil

5 tablespoons fruity extra virgin olive oil

2 strips of lemon peel

2 strips of orange peel

1 lb. ripe red tomatoes, skinned, seeded and chopped*

2 sun-dried tomato halves (in oil), very finely sliced

6 baby globe zucchini, halved, or 2 regular zucchini, halved, thickly sliced, then blanched in salted boiling water

1½ cups ricotta, at room temperature

20 sheets lasagne pasta, spinach or plain

sea salt and freshly ground black pepper

Serves 6

1

Remove the basil leaves from the stems and reserve. Tear up half the leaves and keep the remainder whole. Warm the oil in a small saucepan with the basil stems and citrus peel. Remove and discard the stems and peel.

2

Add the tomatoes, sun-dried tomatoes, salt, and pepper, to the oil, then stir in the zucchini. Heat gently for 1 minute. Stir in the chopped basil just before serving. Season the ricotta.

3

Cook the lasagne in a wide saucepan of salted boiling water until just soft—move and separate the sheets as they cook. (You will need 18 sheets, but some may tear or stick together.) Carefully drain the lasagne, then hang the sheets around the edges of the colander so they don't stick together.

4

To assemble the lasagne, make free-form layers of all the ingredients on each serving plate, dress with any remaining infused oil, and sprinkle with salt and freshly ground pepper.

Note: *Prick the tomatoes all over, put in a bowl and cover with boiling water for 2 minutes. Drain. The skins will slip off easily.*

Variation:

• Use roasted vine cherry tomatoes instead of chopped tomatoes (page 38).

Eggplant mozzarella lasagne

This is a no-bake lasagne. All you have to do is pre-cook the pasta and vegetables (a few hours in advance, if you like), then quickly assemble all the components, reheat, and serve—a sort of lasagne-in-a-hurry. Fresh and healthy, it looks as if you've spent hours on it.

3 garlic cloves, crushed

1 small bunch of basil, stems and leaves separated

½ cup olive oil

20 sheets lasagne pasta, fresh or dried

3 eggplants, sliced lengthwise into 12 slices

2 tablespoons tapenade or sun-dried tomato paste

4 zucchini (yellow and/or green), thinly sliced lengthwise, then blanched in salted boiling water

2 mozzarella, thinly sliced

sea salt and freshly ground black pepper

Serves 6

1

Put the garlic, basil stems, and olive oil in a saucepan and warm through for about 10 minutes to infuse the flavors.

2

Cook the lasagne in a wide saucepan of salted boiling water until just soft—move and separate the sheets as they cook. (You will need 18 sheets, but some may tear or stick together.) Carefully drain the lasagne, then put it into cold water to stop it overcooking or sticking together. Hang the sheets around the edges of the colander so they don't stick together.

3

Brush the eggplant and zucchini slices on both sides with some of the infused oil. Cook in a preheated stove-top grill pan or skillet, turning halfway through cooking, until seared and soft.

4

To assemble, arrange 6 slices of eggplant across a baking tray. Top each slice with a sheet of lasagne, spread a little tapenade or tomato paste on each, then add a slice of zucchini and mozzarella, and a couple of basil leaves. Repeat with all the ingredients, until you have 6 multi-storey piles of pasta, vegetables, and mozzarella. Brush all over with more of the infused oil, cover loosely with foil, and heat through in a preheated oven at 425°F for about 5 minutes or until the cheese begins to melt.

Variations:

• Use oven-dried tomatoes (page 80) instead of sun-dried tomato paste. Alternative layering ingredients include seared aubergine, goat' cheese, prosciutto, and basil; soft cheese, toasted pine nuts, cumin seeds, roasted red bell peppers, and mint.

Spinach gnocchi with basil oil

Gnocchi are wonderful made with spinach or with a mixture of other leaves, such as arugula and sorrel. I've also made them with wild greens, including young nettle tops (don't worry—the sting is eradicated as soon as the leaves hit hot water). Usually, gnocchi are made by rolling pieces of dough off the end of a fork—this version is much easier.

5 oz. baby spinach, well washed

1¾ cups ricotta, drained of excess whey

3 egg yolks

a pinch of ground allspice

1 oz. fresh Parmesan cheese, grated

1 tablespoon all-purpose flour

2 tablespoons semolina

sea salt and freshly ground black pepper

Basil oil:

a small bunch of basil, coarsely chopped

6 tablespoons fruity virgin olive oil

Serves 6

1

To blanch the spinach, plunge into boiling salted water for 2 minutes. Drain, squeeze dry in a cloth, and chop very finely.

2

Put in a bowl with the ricotta, eggs, allspice, Parmesan, flour, semolina, salt, and pepper. Work to a firm dough, adding extra flour if necessary.

3

Roll the dough into a long sausage shape, 1 inch thick. Cut into segments about 1 inch long and put on a lightly floured surface.

4

Mix the basil and oil in a small pitcher.

5

Bring a large saucepan of salted water to a boil, add the prepared gnocchi, and cook for about 2–3 minutes until they rise to the top. Drain, divide between 6 heated plates or bowls, and dress with the basil oil and black pepper.

Indian coconut dhaal

with peas and paneer

This soupy pea dhaal, or lentil stew, is made with coconut milk and paneer, the delicious North Indian curd cheese—use mozzarella if you can't find it. This recipe tastes even better if made the day before, so the flavor of the chiles, leaves, and spices fully penetrate the split peas and cheese.

⅓ cup yellow split peas, or channa dhaal, washed in several changes of cold water

2 teaspoons ground coriander

2 teaspoons cumin seeds

1 teaspoon fenugreek seeds

1 inch cinnamon stick

4 small dried chiles

6 small shallots, sliced

1 teaspoon ground turmeric

2 sprigs curry leaves*

1⅓ cups shelled green peas

1¾ cups canned coconut milk

1 cup paneer cheese* or mozzarella, cubed

1 teaspoon mustard seeds

sea salt and freshly ground black pepper

vegetable oil, for frying

To serve:

1 package pappadams*

hot paprika, to sprinkle

Serves 4-6

*Note: Available from Asian stores

1

Put the yellow split peas in a saucepan with 2¾ cups water, bring to a boil, reduce the heat, and simmer for about 50 minutes, skimming off the froth from time to time.

2

Grind the coriander, cumin, fenugreek, cinnamon, and 1 dried chile in a spice mill or coffee grinder. Heat 2 tablespoons of the oil in a skillet, add the shallots and sauté until soft. Stir in the ground spice mixture and the turmeric and cook until the shallots are golden brown.

3

Transfer to the saucepan of split pea dhaal, add 1 sprig of curry leaves, season well, and simmer for 10 minutes. Stir in the peas, coconut milk, and paneer, then gently simmer the dhaal for about 15 minutes—add extra water if the mixture has thickened too much (it should remain soupy).

4

Heat 2 tablespoons of the vegetable oil in a small skillet, add the mustard seeds, the remaining chiles and curry leaves, and sauté for a few seconds. Add to the dhaal and serve in 1 large bowl or divide between 4 or 6 small bowls.

5

Wipe out the small pan, pour in 1-inch depth of the vegetable oil and heat until a small piece of pappadam or bread browns in 30 seconds. Fry the pappadams, one by one, until crisp. Remove, drain, sprinkle with hot paprika, and serve with the dhaal.

Corn and sweet potato bhajia

with sambal dip

Bhajia are delicious vegetable fitters from Indonesia and India. Don't be put off by the long list of ingredients—everything is easily put together. Sambal isn't compulsory, but it's delicious and contains all the flavors of Indonesian cooking, salt, hot, sour, and sweet (you could always use soy sauce instead).

3 fresh corn cobs

1 large sweet potato, finely sliced or grated

⅔ cup all-purpose flour

12 scallions, finely sliced lengthwise

4 small shallots, finely sliced

3 tablespoons chopped fresh cilantro

1½ inches fresh ginger, grated

1 garlic clove, crushed

2 small red chiles

1 teaspoon sugar

vegetable oil, for frying

Sambal dip:

1 stalk lemongrass, trimmed and finely chopped

1 garlic clove, crushed

3 red chiles, finely sliced

1 teaspoon shrimp paste (*blachan*)*, (optional)

1 tablespoon peanut oil

3 teaspoons caster sugar

4 tomatoes, seeded and chopped

2 tablespoons *kecap manis* (Indonesian ketchup)* or dark soy sauce

1 tablespoon tamarind paste* mixed with 3 tablespoons water or 2 tablespoons lime juice with 2 tablespoons water

1 tablespoon crushed toasted peanuts, to serve (optional)

Serves 6

1

To make the sambal, mix the lemongrass with the garlic, chiles, and shrimp paste and sauté in the peanut oil for about 1 minute. Stir in the remaining ingredients. Let cool. Serve in a small dish, sprinkled with crushed toasted peanuts, if using.

2

Meanwhile, to make the bhajia, first cook the corn in a large saucepan of boiling water for 8 minutes. Drain, then hold the corn vertically on a board and slice off the kernels. Discard the core.

3

Mix the corn, sweet potato, flour, shallots, scallions, cilantro, ginger, garlic, chiles, and sugar in a bowl. Add ½ cup warm water and stir to form a thick batter.

4

Heat the oil in a large skillet, add tablespoons of the mixture and sauté in small batches until golden on both sides. Drain on crumpled paper towels. Serve the bhajia with a small dish of the sambal.

Note: *Available at Asian specialty markets.*

Green tomato and basil curry

This is a Thai, souplike curry. The sharpness of the tart green tomatoes is perfect with the sweet and salt flavors of the curry. If green tomatoes are unavailable, use underripe ones instead, adding them to the pan about 5 minutes before the end of cooking.

1½ lb. green tomatoes, quartered

a handful of basil leaves, chopped, plus extra for serving

5 tablespoons extra virgin olive oil

2¾ cups canned coconut milk

1 tablespoon fish sauce*

2 teaspoons sugar

sea salt and freshly ground black pepper

Curry paste:

4 large mild green chiles, chopped

5 hot green chiles, chopped

5 shallots, chopped

5 garlic cloves

1½ inches ginger, chopped

1 stalk lemongrass, trimmed, outer casing discarded, chopped

6 kaffir lime leaves*, finely chopped, or 1 teaspoon finely chopped lime zest

2 teaspoons shrimp paste (*blachan*)*, or anchovy essence

Serves 4–6

Note: Available at Asian specialty markets. Shrimp paste is a salty Indonesian seasoning. If unavailable, omit it or use anchovy essence.

1

Put all the ingredients for the curry paste into a food processor or blender and work to a paste. Add 2 of the quartered tomatoes and purée again.

2

Mix the chopped basil in a bowl with 3 tablespoons of the olive oil.

3

Heat the remaining oil in a wok or wide, shallow saucepan, add the paste, and stir-fry until the oil separates—about 4 minutes.

4

Add the coconut milk, fish sauce, sugar, salt, pepper, and 1¾ cups water. Bring to a boil, reduce the heat, and simmer for about 15 minutes. Add the tomato quarters and gently simmer for a further 10 minutes. Stir in the basil-flavored oil and serve with whole basil leaves on top—and plenty of plain boiled rice.

Variations:

• Before serving, you could stir in some fresh pesto, made without Parmesan—the creamy pine nuts add an extra dimension to the taste and texture, not dissimilar to the crushed nuts used in many Asian curry pastes.

• Add thin strips of stir-fried beef or chicken and other vegetables, such as Thai wing beans or dwarf beans. Use cilantro instead of basil.

• Make a red tomato curry using red tomato and red chiles instead of green, adding whole cherry tomatoes 5 minutes before the end of cooking.

Pumpkin coconut curry

Make this curry with ordinary pumpkin, or with spaghetti squash—melon-shaped, with yellow flesh that pulls into strands when cooked. I prefer to bake it first before adding to the curry, to retain the long strands.

1½ lb. pumpkin or spaghetti squash, peeled, seeded, and cut into chunks

10 small shallots, finely sliced lengthwise

4 garlic cloves, crushed

½ teaspoon turmeric

1½ inches fresh ginger, chopped

2 stalks lemongrass, finely chopped

1 tablespoon red Thai curry paste

3 tablespoons salted cashews

4 tablespoons peanut oil, plus extra for brushing

1 teaspoon tamarind paste
or 1 tablespoon fresh lemon juice

1¾ cups canned coconut milk

1 cup chicken or vegetable stock

sea salt

To serve:

fresh cilantro leaves

fresh bean sprouts

Serves 6

1

If using spaghetti squash, brush it with a little oil and salt, then bake in a preheated oven at 375°F for 30–45 minutes until cooked. Pull the flesh into strings. If using regular pumpkin, cut it into bite-sized chunks.

2

Place 4 shallots, the garlic, turmeric, ginger, lemongrass, Thai curry paste, and cashews into an electric blender and process to a coarse paste.

3

Heat 2 tablespoons of the oil in a skillet, add the paste, and sauté until it darkens, adding a drop more oil if required. Add the tamarind or lemon juice, pumpkin or squash, coconut milk, and stock and simmer for 10 minutes or until the pumpkin is tender.

4

Heat the remaining oil in a second skillet, add the remaining shallots and sauté until crisp. Spread out on paper towels to drain. Sprinkle well with salt.

5

Divide the pumpkin or squash between 6 bowls and serve topped with sautéed shallots, cilantro, and bean sprouts.

Indian spiced eggplant

with egg, basil, and cardamom rice

The eggplant take on a mildly spiced sweet and sour flavor. Eat it hot or cold —(it's wonderful either way) or serve with freshly baked focaccia instead of rice, and you have great picnic food. Cook ahead, if you can, and leave for a few hours for the flavors to develop and meld—reheat before serving.

1 inch fresh ginger, chopped

6 garlic cloves

1 onion, chopped

3 medium eggplants, quartered lengthwise, with the central "seed" core removed

½ cup mustard oil, peanut or corn oil, for sauteing, plus 1 tablespoon extra

2 teaspoons ground cumin

2 teaspoons lightly crushed coriander seeds

3 teaspoons panchphoran spice mix*

a pinch of cayenne pepper

4 tomatoes, chopped

3 tablespoons red wine vinegar

4 teaspoons brown sugar

a handful of fresh basil leaves

8 cardamom pods

2 cups basmati rice

sea salt and freshly ground black pepper

4 hard-cooked eggs, peeled and halved, to serve

Serves 6

1

Put the ginger, garlic, and onion in a food processor and work to a coarse paste.

2

Sprinkle the eggplants with salt and pepper. Heat ½ cup of the oil in a skillet, add half the cumin and coriander seeds and the eggplant. Sauté on all sides until lightly golden. Put the eggplant in a colander over a bowl.

3

Tip any collected oil from the eggplant back into the skillet, heat and add the panchphoran. Sauté for a few seconds until the seeds pop. Add the ginger paste, cayenne, and the remaining cumin and coriander seeds and sauté until the oil separates from the mixture, (adding extra oil if necessary). Add the tomatoes, vinegar, and sugar and cook gently for about 10 minutes, stirring occasionally to prevent sticking.

4

Add the fried eggplant to the mixture and cook for a further 5–10 minutes. Add salt and pepper to taste. Keep hot and stir in half the basil just before serving.

5

Heat 1 tablespoon of oil in a deep saucepan, add the cardamom pods, and sauté until aromatic. Add the rice and stir to coat the grains with oil. Add salt and 3 cups water, cover, and bring to a boil. Reduce the heat and simmer very gently for 8 minutes. Turn off the heat and leave covered for 10 minutes.

6

Spoon the rice into 6 heated bowls, then top with the eggplants, the remaining basil, and the halved, hard-cooked eggs.

Variations:

• Use cilantro or mint instead of basil.

• Add fresh curry leaves to flavor the curry or along with the cardamom to flavor the rice.

• Serve the pickled eggplant with pappadams (Indian crispbreads) instead of rice or stir a spoonful of melted creamed coconut into the rice just before serving.

Note: *Panchphoran is available from Indian stores. If you can't find it, make your own: mix 2 teaspoons each of black mustard seeds, cumin seeds, nigella (onion) seeds, fennel seeds, and fenugreek seeds—it's not imperative that you include all of these, but "panch" means "five" in Hindi.*

Pot-roasted red onions

with feta cheese and oregano

Peeled red onions are slow-baked with oregano and olive oil, then served with crumbled feta cheese. I'm not a big fan of quartered roast onions—they over-caramelize and taste too burnt at the edges. Baking or roasting them whole keeps them succulent and makes the bulbs meltingly tender, full of onion concentrate. You can swap oregano for rosemary, and you can take it even further if you like—see the variations below.

12 small or 6 medium red onions

2 teaspoons dried oregano

4 tablespoons olive oil

12 black olives

leaves from 4 sprigs of oregano

1 cup feta or blue cheese, crumbled

sea salt and freshly ground black pepper

Serves 6

1

Stand the peeled onions in a snug-fitting casserole (with lid) or a roasting pan (use foil as a cover). Sprinkle with dried oregano, spoon over half of the oil, and season generously. Cover and roast in a preheated oven at 350°F for 45–60 minutes or until tender.

2

Remove the lid, put in the olives and a few of the fresh oregano leaves, baste with the remaining olive oil, and return to the oven for 5 minutes. Serve with crumbled feta or blue cheese and the remaining oregano leaves.

Variations:

• Slice the roasted onions into quarters before serving and toss with all the ingredients, plus winter salad leaves, walnuts, a dash of walnut oil, and balsamic vinegar.

• Cut in half lengthwise and put cut side up in a gratin dish. Baste with garlic-infused olive oil and herbs, then lightly caramelize under a hot broiler. Serve with mashed sweet potato and broiled lamb cutlets or pork chops.

Thyme buttered baby roots

with homemade horseradish cream

This dish of perfectly cooked tender little roots—tails, tops, and all—is good enough as a course on its own. You can also use grown-up roots, cut to size. Hamburg parsley tastes and looks like baby parsnip, but has a more earthy herby flavor. Salsify is a long narrow hairy root, not the most endearing of objects, but with delicious creamy flesh.

¼ cup butter

4 sprigs of thyme

sea salt and freshly ground black pepper

A selection of baby roots, such as:

baby waxy potatoes, unpeeled but scrubbed

baby carrots, unpeeled, trimmed, and scrubbed

baby turnips, scrubbed or peeled if larger

Hamburg parsley root, peeled

salsify or scorzonera, peeled*

rutabaga, peeled and cut into chunks

small parsnips, peeled

Jerusalem artichokes, peeled and cut into chunks*

Homemade horseradish and garlic cream (optional):

5 tablespoons crème fraîche or sour cream

1 tablespoon freshly grated horseradish root

2 shallots, finely chopped

2 garlic cloves, crushed

2 tablespoons white wine vinegar

salt and freshly ground black pepper

Serves 6

Note: *Peeled salsify and Jerusalem artichokes should be put into a bowl of acidulated water (water with a dash of lemon juice) to prevent browning. Dip in the lemon water as you peel; it will stop your hands from staining too.*

1

Put all the horseradish cream ingredients in a bowl and beat well. Taste and add a dash more vinegar or seasoning if necessary.

2

Melt the butter and strip the thyme leaves from their stems into the butter and leave to infuse while you cook the roots.

3

Simmer the prepared roots in salted water until cooked (pierce a large one with a knife to test). If certain roots are larger or thicker than others (such as parsnips), start off with them first, and cook for about 8 minutes, then add the smaller, narrower ones (such as baby carrots) and let simmer for a further 3 minutes. Drain and toss with the thyme butter, sea salt, and black pepper. Serve with a spoonful of horseradish cream, if using.

Variations:

• Serve thyme buttered roots with:

• Salt beef (poached until tender with carrots, onion, bay leaf, and peppercorns) and freshly grated horseradish.

• Beet aioli (mayonnaise mixed with crushed garlic and cooked puréed beets).

• Clay Pot Lemon Poussin (page 104).

• Roast rib of beef (include the horseradish and garlic cream) or with other roasted meats.

Porcini pizza with garlic butter

Porcini—"little pigs" in Italian—are also known as cepes and are the kings of the mushroom family. Their flavor is rich and intense—the very essence of mushroominess. Don't make this with dried porcini, which should only be used in sauces, stocks, and braises. Use other wild mushrooms instead.

½ cup butter

14 oz. fresh porcini, sliced, or other wild mushrooms, wiped clean and woody stem ends removed

3 garlic cloves, crushed

2 mozzarella, thinly sliced

3 sprigs of rosemary

sea salt and freshly ground black pepper

Pizza dough:

½ oz. fresh yeast

3½ cups *tipo 00* flour or all-purpose flour

1 teaspoon salt

a pinch of sugar

fine semolina, for dusting

Makes 4 or 12 pizzette

1

To make the pizza dough, dissolve the yeast in 1 cup warm water. Pile the flour on a work surface and make a well in the center. Add the yeast mixture, salt, and sugar. Mix to a soft dough, then knead until silky and elastic. Dust with flour, put in a bowl, cover, and leave in a warm place for about 1 hour until doubled in size.

2

To make the topping, heat the butter in a wide skillet, add the sliced porcini and sauté briefly on both sides. Stir in the garlic and seasoning and remove from the heat. Heat a lightly oiled, heavy baking tray in the oven, set at its highest setting, until very hot.

3

Punch down the risen dough with your knuckles and divide into 4 or 12 pieces. Flatten each with a rolling pin and, using your fingers (or rolling pin), stretch into long flat oval shapes. Dust on both sides with semolina. Brush with the garlic butter, sprinkle with slices of mozzarella, and top with the porcini and the leaves from the sprigs of rosemary. Arrange on the preheated baking tray and bake at the same temperature for 10–15 minutes for large or 8 minutes for small.

We're still a little afraid when it comes to cooking fish. And at the fish counter many of us are unsure of what to ask for. For some, it's difficult to imagine how to transform a whole fish—head, fins, tail, and all—into four elegant portions on the dinner table. But don't be embarrassed to ask any questions you like—a lot of people in the line behind you haven't much of a clue either.

If you like fish, you really like it, as I do. A fresh fish rubbed with seasoning, herbs, and olive oil, and seared until crisp on the outside and just cooked within tastes fantastic. It's also very good for you and takes minutes to cook, which makes it my kind of food. But it has to be very fresh. So when picking out your fish look for bright clear eyes and blood-free, pink gills and ask the fishmonger when it was caught.

There is one snag with fish and that's the bones. If there's one thing that can put us off eating fish, it must be the idea of all those fiddly little bones to deal with. But there's a way out of this—buy fillets of fish. If the fish counter has no filleted fish then don't hesitate to ask for a whole fish to be cleaned and filleted for you. A cinch to prepare, as fast as a burger to cook— and 100% better for you—and the big plus, no bones. Just rub, crust, bathe, or wrap, then sear, grill, or roast.

Freshness is all-important for shellfish too. When it comes to mussels, and clams, always throw out ones that remain open after you have scrubbed them. Then discard any that remain closed after they have been cooked. If you are cooking from fresh, all crustacea (excluding shrimp), including lobsters and crabs should be live.

fish and seafood

Chile crisp shrimp and garlic chives with wasabi mayonnaise

Maybe I'm unusual in my desire to eat shrimp unpeeled, but their shells turn crispy when blistered and take on the caramelized lime and chile-garlic flavors in the pan. Garlic chives taste faintly spicy with a garlic-onion flavor. You can also use ordinary chives, scallions, or wild garlic leaves.

3–4 teaspoons wasabi paste*

6 tablespoons mayonnaise

12 whole uncooked jumbo shrimp

2 stalks lemongrass, trimmed, outer layers discarded, inside layers finely sliced

1 teaspoon chile flakes

2 garlic cloves, chopped

1 tablespoon fish sauce

2 teaspoons sugar

2 tablespoons lime juice, preferably from kaffir limes

2 teaspoons grated lime zest

1 bunch Chinese garlic chives, some finely scissor-snipped, others left whole

sea salt

corn or peanut oil, for cooking

Serves 6

Note: Wasabi paste (hot Japanese horseradish) is sold in tubes, bottles, or powder form in larger supermarkets and Asian shops.

1

Beat the wasabi and mayonnaise together. Spoon into small dishes.

2

Mix the shrimp with the lemongrass, chile flakes, garlic, fish sauce, sugar, lime juice, and zest.

3

Heat 1 tablespoon of the oil in a heavy-bottom skillet, add the shrimp and sprinkle generously with sea salt. Sear on both sides until the shells are caramelized and brittle and the flesh opaque.

4

Toss the snipped chives with the shrimp and serve on a bed of whole garlic chives.

5

To eat, remove the head and legs, dip the shrimp into the wasabi mayonnaise and eat them whole, including the crispy shells.

Variations:

Chile crisp shrimp also go with:

• Noodles and extra chopped garlic chives.

• Stir-fried greens and extra garlic chives.

• Salad leaves.

71

Seafood and corn gumbo

Gumbo is the Louisiana classic thickened with filé (ground sassafras leaves) or chopped okra and usually made with seafood, although chicken, duck, and boudin sausage can be used too. My version is more like a *marinière* (no self-respecting Louisiana cook would add wine)—but it tastes wonderful anyway.

2 lb. mixed seafood, such as mussels or clams, calamari, shrimp, or lobster

2 fresh corn cobs

4 tablespoons olive oil

1 teaspoon chile flakes

4 garlic cloves, crushed

4 shallots, chopped

3 carrots, diced

2 teaspoons coriander seeds

1¼ cups white wine

2¾ cups chicken stock

juice of 1 lime

a pinch of saffron

6 tomatoes, quartered

½ lb. okra

2 tablespoons chopped parsley

1 tablespoon chopped thyme

sea salt and freshly ground black pepper

To serve:

fresh cilantro sprigs

char-grilled bread or boiled rice

Serves 6

1

Scrub the mussels or clams and discard any that remain open.

2

Boil the corn in unsalted water for about 8 minutes and either cut into chunks or slice the kernels off the cobs.

3

Put the calamari, shrimp, if using, and 1 tablespoon of the oil in a bowl with the chile flakes, salt, pepper, and half the garlic. Heat a skillet until smoking hot and sear the calamari and shrimp or lobster for 1 minute. Remove from the skillet and set aside.

4

Heat the remaining oil in the skillet, add the shallots, carrots, coriander seeds, and remaining garlic and sauté until softened but not browned. Add the wine, stock, lime juice, and saffron and simmer for 5 minutes. Add the mussels or clams, corn, tomatoes, and okra and simmer gently for a further 5 minutes. Add the remaining seafood, parsley, and thyme, then taste and adjust the seasoning. Cook for a further 2 minutes.

5

Divide the gumbo between 6 heated bowls, top with cilantro and serve with char-grilled bread or boiled rice.

Shrimp and eggplant laksa

Pea eggplants, sold in Thai stores, are pea-sized and grow in bunches. They have a tart taste and light crunch. A laksa is a Malay curry with noodles. It can be kept simple with just rice vermicelli noodles and fresh herbs or made more elaborate, by adding seafood, fishcakes, and condiments.

½ cup peanut or corn oil

1 stalk lemongrass, trimmed and smashed

3½ cups canned coconut milk

a handful of pea eggplants or fresh peas

7 oz. rice vermicelli noodles

juice of ½ lime

12 large cooked shrimp

sea salt and freshly ground black pepper

fresh cilantro, to serve

Rempah:

⅓ cup macadamia or cashews

8 small shallots, chopped

4 garlic cloves, crushed

2 small red chillies, chopped

1 inch fresh turmeric root, peeled and chopped (optional)*

1 inch fresh ginger or galangal, chopped

2 teaspoons chopped cilantro root or 1 teaspoon coriander seeds

1 teaspoon shrimp paste (*blachan*) or anchovy essence

Serves 6

1

Put all the rempah ingredients in a blender or food processor and blend to a paste. Heat the oil in a saucepan or wok, add the paste and stir-fry until darkened. Strain off the excess oil.

2

Add the lemongrass, coconut milk, and ¾ cup water. Bring to a fast simmer until reduced and thickened a little. Add the pea eggplants or peas and simmer gently for about 10 minutes.

3

Soak the rice noodles in a bowl of hot water until soft—about 15 minutes. Drain and divide between 6 bowls.

4

Season the soup with the lime juice, salt, and pepper, then ladle over the noodles. Add plenty of fresh cilantro and 2 shrimp to each bowl.

__Note:__ Turmeric root is available from Asian markets. It doesn't have a great deal of flavor and is mainly used for its color. The dazzling ocher-colored juices stain everything, including fingers—so handle with care.

Variations:

• Other cooked seafood, such as calamari, octopus, fish pieces, crispy fishcakes, mussels, or clams can be added.

• Cooked sliced meat or poultry, spicy meat balls or poached egg, other vegetables, crisp shallots, and Asian herbs can be added.

75

Lemon herb-cured salmon trout with dill potatoes

Home curing is easier than you think. Sprinkle the fish with the ingredients, wrap and chill for 2 days. That's all—just remember to start 2 days before you want to eat it. The salmon trout is delicious with this potato salad but is also great served on buttered toast with a good squeeze of lemon juice.

1 salmon or salmon trout, 3 lb., filleted (skin-on)

3 tablespoons sea salt

3 tablespoons sugar

2 teaspoons lemon zest

2 tablespoons akvavit or vodka

1 bunch of dill, chopped

1 bunch of chives, chopped

1 bunch of flat-leaf parsley, chopped

1 bunch of chervil, chopped

1 bunch of basil, chopped

young salad leaves, to serve

Dill potato salad:

2 tablespoons finely chopped red onion

2 tablespoons white wine vinegar

2 teaspoons sugar

2 tablespoons chopped fresh dill

1 tablespoon fresh lemon juice

1 lb. baby new potatoes, boiled and cooled

4 tablespoons sour cream

2 teaspoons freshly grated horseradish

sea salt and freshly ground black pepper

Serves 4–6

1

Put the fillets, skin side down, on a large piece of plastic wrap. Remove any pin bones (they run down the lateral line). Mix the salt, sugar, lemon zest, akvavit or vodka, dill, chives, parsley, chervil, and basil in a bowl, then press onto the flesh. Wrap tightly in plastc, put on a shallow tray, and weigh down. Refrigerate for 1 day, then turn it over and refrigerate again. After 2 days, unwrap and rinse off the curing ingredients with cold running water. Pat dry with paper towels. Cover with more finely chopped herbs, then wrap in plastic until just before serving.

2

To make the potato salad, put the onion in a bowl with the wine vinegar, sugar, dill, lemon juice, salt, and pepper. Marinate for 20 minutes, then add the potatoes, sour cream, and horseradish. Serve in 1 large or 4 or 6 small bowls.

3

Finely slice the salmon crosswise into strips, leaving the skin behind. Serve on a bed of leaves.

Pastrami salmon with caraway celery root

The salmon is flavored with pastrami-cure style ingredients: it semi-cures overnight. If you want to inject loads of flavor, leave the spices and herbs on for a further day or two, but even just 2–4 hours works wonders. Salmon also loves salt (it brings out the flavor and firms up the flesh) and when seared until blackened on both sides, the flavors are intensified. Freshly grated celery root can be bought in pillow packs from speciality shops

2 lb. salmon fillet (middle cut of a large salmon), skin on, pin bones removed

1 tablespoon olive oil

Pastrami cure:

1 tablespoon salt

1 tablespoon sugar

1 teaspoon ground allspice

1 teaspoon paprika

1 teaspoon garlic powder

1 teaspoon onion powder

1 tablespoon whole-grain or mild mustard

2 tablespoons finely chopped chives

2 tablespoons finely chopped dill, plus a few sprigs, to serve

Caraway celery root:

1 celery root (celeriac), about 1 lb.

juice of 1 lemon

2 tablespoons butter

1 shallot, finely chopped

1 teaspoon caraway seeds

½ cup white wine

⅔ cup double cream

1 teaspoon mustard powder

salt and freshly ground black pepper

1

To make the pastrami cure, mix all the ingredients in a bowl. Rub it over the flesh side of the salmon, wrap tightly in plastic, put in a shallow dish, weight down with a food can, and chill overnight.

2

To prepare the celery root, peel it, cut in quarters, and dip in a bowl of water with half the lemon juice to prevent browning. Using a food processor or mandoline, cut into long, fine julienne strips (a normal grater will give you a mush) and immerse in the acidulated water.

3

Drain the celery root. Heat the butter in a small skillet, add the shallot, and sauté until soft and translucent. Add salt, pepper, and caraway seeds and cook for 1 minute without browning. Add the wine and remaining lemon juice and reduce until syrupy. Stir in the cream, mustard powder, and celery root and gently cook until just softened, about 3 minutes. Taste and adjust the seasoning.

4

Scrape the pastrami cure off the salmon and rub with the oil. Heat a heavy-bottom skillet until smoking hot (turn on the extraction fan) and sear the fillet, skin side down, for about 3 minutes. Don't move it—it's meant to blacken, but won't taste burnt. Slide a spatula under the fish, turn it over and sear for 2 minutes. It should be opaque and undercooked in the middle. Slice into 6 and serve with the caraway celery root.

Serves 6

Blackened salmon

with oven-roasted tomato salad

I like my salmon undercooked. Opaque, moist, and succulent. And this is it—perfect salmon in a matter of minutes. Serve it warm or at room temperature. Oven-roasted tomatoes taste like a cross between roasted and sun-dried tomatoes; the slow drying process concentrates the tomato taste and much improves fresh tomatoes low on flavor.

12 plum tomatoes, quartered

6 teaspoons dried oregano

1½ lb. thick salmon fillet, skin on

2 teaspoons paprika

1 garlic clove, crushed

sea salt and freshly ground black pepper

olive oil, for brushing

Dressing:

6 tablespoons extra virgin olive oil

1½ teaspoons balsamic vinegar

Serves 6

1

Put the quartered tomatoes on a baking tray lined with parchment paper. Sprinkle with half the oregano, salt, and pepper, and brush with olive oil. Put onto the bottom shelf of the oven and set to 200ºF. Let dry for about 2–3 hours. Check them occasionally in case they dry too fast.

2

Rub the flesh side of the salmon fillet with the remaining oregano, paprika, garlic, salt, and pepper, and then brush all over with olive oil.

3

Heat a heavy iron skillet (preferably nonstick) until smoking hot. Add the salmon, flesh side down, and sear without moving it for 2 minutes. Turn it over (it should look blackened) and cook for a further 3 minutes; it should be rare in the middle. Remove the skin and flake the flesh into large chunks.

4

To serve, put the flaked salmon and the oven-roasted tomatoes on 6 plates. Mix the dressing ingredients together and sprinkle over each serving.

Variations:

• Add torn lettuce leaves, such as batavia (escarole) or romaine, chopped avocado, and fine beans.

• Serve with the tapenade cannellini beans (page 38).

• Use oven-roasted tomatoes with broiled vegetables and basil to make a ratatouille salad, or use them in Eggplant Mozzarella Lasagne (page 48).

Steamed sea bass

with snowpeas and soy beans

Slice some ginger, garlic, and scallions, set the fish on its bed of snowpeas and black soy beans, and you're there—10 minutes is all it takes. If you're not keen on handling (or for that matter seeing) a whole fish—with head, fins, tail, and all—on your table, then ask your fishmonger to fillet it for you then put the two fillets together before cooking.

1 whole sea bass, about 2 lb., cleaned, scaled, and washed

2 garlic cloves, sliced

3 inches fresh ginger, finely sliced

4 scallions, trimmed, halved, and shredded

½ tablespoon light soy sauce

4 teaspoons sesame oil

sea salt and crushed Szechuan peppercorns or black pepper

2 large handfuls of snowpeas

2 tablespoons whole black soy beans (drained if in brine), rinsed*

sprigs of cilantro or Thai basil leaves, to serve

Serves 4

Note: Salted black soy beans are available from Asian grocers. Drain and rinse off excess salt before using.

1
Season the fish inside and out with salt and pepper and tuck half the garlic and ginger into the cavity.

2
Lay the fish on parchment paper. Sprinkle the scallions and the remaining ginger and garlic on top. Drizzle with the soy sauce and half the sesame oil.

3
Fold over the paper to enclose the fish and crease the edges together. Place in a steamer or oven preheated to 400°F and cook for 10 minutes.

4
Heat the remaining oil in a wok or large skillet, add the snowpeas and black beans, and stir-fry for about 1 minute.

5
To serve, put the snowpeas and beans on a warmed serving plate, lay the fish on top, and pour over any cooking juices. Sprinkle with the herbs and serve.

Bacon-wrapped monkfish

with Brussels tops and horseradish picada

Monkfish is a deep sea fish with a dense meaty flesh that's ideal for roasting. Brussels tops are the young leaves that crown sprout plants. They're sweet and very tender and don't taste at all sproutlike. If you can't find them, use spring greens or cabbage instead.

6 monkfish fillets,
about 3 lb. in total

12 slices bacon

6 Brussels tops,
coarse stems removed

1 tablespoon balsamic vinegar

2 tablespoons olive oil,
plus extra for brushing

sea salt and freshly ground
black pepper

Horseradish picada:

⅓ cup olive oil, or to taste

⅓ cup skinned hazelnuts*

⅓ cup skinned almonds*

1 thick slice white bread

½ tablespoon sherry vinegar

2 tablespoons raisins,
soaked in sherry vinegar

3 tablespoons
creamed horseradish

sea salt and freshly ground
black pepper

Serves 6

Note: To skin nuts, soak for a few minutes in boiling water, then pop them out of their brown skins (almonds) or wrap them in a cloth and rub them off (hazelnuts).

1

To make the picada, heat 1 tablespoon of the oil in a skillet, add the nuts, and gently sauté until lightly browned. Remove, and sauté the bread in the same oil. Put the nuts, bread, salt, and pepper in a food processor and blend to a paste. With the motor running, slowly add olive oil in a thin stream until the paste becomes a thick sauce. Stir in vinegar to taste, then add the raisins and horseradish. Set aside.

2

Lightly sprinkle the monkfish with salt and pepper, wrap each piece in 2 bacon slices and put into a roasting pan. Brush the wrapped fish with olive oil and put the pan on top of the stove. Cook over a high heat until lightly brown all over. Transfer to a preheated oven and roast at 425°F for 8–10 minutes. Remove from the oven. If the bacon has not crisped, brown under a hot broiler.

3

Half fill a wok with water, then add salt and pepper. Bring to a boil, add the prepared Brussels tops, and blanch for 1 minute. Drain off the water, then add the vinegar and 2 tablespoons olive oil, more salt and pepper, and stir-fry for a further 1 minute.

4

Divide the wilted Brussels tops between 6 wide, shallow bowls. Slice each piece of monkfish into 4 and place on top of the wilted leaves. Serve with a spoonful of picada.

Fish fillets in beer batter

with pea purée and mint vinaigrette

Delicious pea purée is sometimes made from dried peas, but here I have made it with fresh peas. I used monkfish, a cartilaginous fish which has no fine bones and so is easy to eat. If you can't find one, substitute another fish—cod or flounder would be good—but remove any pin bones.

6 pieces of monkfish, skate, cod or flounder, about 7 oz. each

sea salt

sunflower or vegetable oil, for deep-frying

Beer batter:

1⅓ cups all-purpose flour, plus extra to dust

½ teaspoon sea salt

2 teaspoons baking powder

1 cup beer

2 egg whites

Pea purée:

3 tablespoons unsalted butter

1 onion, chopped

1 thick slice of bacon

2½ cups shelled peas

Mint vinaigrette:

½ teaspoon sugar

leaves from 1 bunch mint, chopped

4 tablespoons virgin olive oil

2 tablespoons lemon juice

1 tablespoon balsamic vinegar

sea salt and freshly ground black pepper

Serves 6

1

To make the batter, sieve the flour, salt, and baking powder in a bowl. Stir in the beer and set aside for 30 minutes. Beat the egg whites to soft peak stage and mix in just before using.

2

To make the pea purée, melt the butter in a saucepan, add the onion, and cook gently until softened and translucent, about 5–10 minutes. Add the bacon and peas and cover with water (do not salt). Bring to a boil, reduce the heat, and simmer for 10 minutes. Discard the bacon, put the peas in a food processor, add salt and pepper to taste, then work to a purée. Set aside to keep warm.

3

To make the mint vinaigrette, beat the sugar, mint, oil, lemon juice, vinegar, salt, and pepper in a pitcher or bowl.

4

Fill a saucepan or wok one-third full of oil, heat to 375°F, or until a cube of bread browns in 30 seconds. Season and dust the fish with flour, dip in the batter, and deep-fry in the oil until golden, about 4–5 minutes.

5

Serve with a spoonful of pea purée and mint vinaigrette.

Salmon fish fingers

with asparagus, spring peas, and mustard-mint butter

This asparagus mixture is wonderful on its own as an appetizer—or with fish, meat, or poultry as an entrée. Vary the ingredients according to whatever is fresh and exciting in the market.

Fish fingers:

6 salmon fillets, 6 oz. each

¾ cup couscous

1 garlic clove, crushed

grated zest of 1 lemon

1 teaspoon paprika

1 teaspoon ground cumin

1 teaspoon ground coriander

1 teaspoon ground ginger

flour, for dusting

2 eggs, lightly beaten

sea salt and pepper

butter and olive oil, for cooking

30 asparagus tips

6 small green or yellow zucchini, halved

9 oz. mixed spring peas or beans

5 tablespoons butter

1 tablespoon whole-grain mustard

chopped fresh mint and chives, to serve

Serves 6

1

To make the fish fingers, pat the salmon dry with paper towels. Put the couscous in a bowl, add boiling water until just covered, then set aside for 5 minutes until doubled in size. Fluff up with a fork, leave 5 minutes more, then fluff up again. Spread out on a wide plate and let dry for 10 minutes. Mix with the garlic, lemon zest, paprika, cumin, coriander, ginger, salt, and pepper. Dip the fish in flour, then in beaten egg, then in the couscous mixture—pat on extra. Chill for 2 minutes.

2

Blanch the asparagus, pattypans, zucchini, or beans, if using, in boiling salted water for 1–2 minutes. Add the sugar snaps or snowpeas, if using, and blanch for 1 minute more.

3

Heat the butter and oil in skillet, add the fish and sauté gently for 2 minutes on each side. Remove and drain on paper towels.

4

Heat the butter and mustard in a large, shallow skillet or wok, add the drained vegetables, and toss well. Heat through for about 1 minute, then toss in the mint.

5

To serve, slice each fillet lengthwise to make 2 "fingers." Put 2 pieces of fish on each plate, and pile the mustard buttered vegetables on top. Sprinkle with chives and serve.

Smoked fishcakes

with lemon butter spinach

Smoked fish makes the best fishcakes. Other fish such as salmon often seem tasteless when mixed with mashed potato and sautéed. I've made champ, the Irish dish of mashed potato infused with scallion, as the base for my cakes. The lemon butter is much easier to make than hollandaise.

1¼ cups milk

1 lb. smoked haddock

2 tablespoons butter

4 scallions, finely chopped

3 tablespoons heavy cream

1¾ lb. potatoes, cooked in boiling salted water

2 tablespoons chopped parsley

freshly grated nutmeg

all-purpose flour, for dusting

1 egg, lightly beaten

¼ cup breadcrumbs (from day-old white bread)

vegetable oil, for frying

sea salt and freshly ground black pepper

Lemon butter spinach:

juice of 1 lemon

6 tablespoons butter, chilled and diced

baby spinach, to serve

Makes 12 balls or 6 cakes

1

Heat the milk in a wide, shallow saucepan, add the haddock, and poach for about 5 minutes. Remove from the milk and let cool. Flake the fish, removing any bones and skin. Discard the milk.

2

Heat the butter in a small saucepan over a gentle heat, add the scallions and cream, and sauté gently for about 1 minute to soften the scallions. Add the mixture to the cooked potato and mash them together. Add the parsley, nutmeg, salt, and pepper. Mix in the flaked fish, taste and adjust the seasoning, then chill for 1 hour or overnight to firm the mixture.

3

Mold the fish and potato mixture into 12 small balls or 6 large cakes. Flour each cake, dip into the beaten egg, and then pat with breadcrumbs. Chill until needed.

4

Heat the vegetable oil in a deep-fat fryer to the recommended level and temperature. Add the balls in batches and deep-fry for about 3 minutes. Alternatively, heat about ½-inch depth of oil and 1 tablespoon of butter in a large, preferably nonstick, skillet. Add the fishcakes and sauté all over until golden brown. Set aside to keep them warm.

5

Gently heat the lemon juice in a small saucepan and beat in the chilled butter over a low heat to form an emulsion. Toss with the spinach and serve with the fishcakes.

chicken and

other birds

Birds are creatures of pleasurable contrast. The cooked breast meat is different from the leg, and the crispy skin is something else, be it chicken or duck. It's this "else" that I can't get enough of. Chicken has great lean meat, the breast is white and, if correctly cooked, succulent, while the legs are dark and almost creamy. And everything, when roasted, is jacketed in the most sought after (and fought over) crinkle-crisp, salty skin. One of the best ways to keep the breast meat of chicken moist is to pot-roast it.

Duck on the other hand is best pricked all over, rubbed with salt and open-roasted on a rack as it has to shed a lot of fat as it cooks. You needn't worry about it drying out, the fat seems to constantly lubricate the meat as it melts. Other gamebirds are best pot-roasted, with the addition of some liquid, plus some wine or something fortified, and this will keep them plump and flavorsome.

Years ago when I worked for Habitat, they sold a thing called a chicken brick. This was a rounded clay pot made up of two halves that neatly slotted together and entombed the bird. The brick sealed in all the juices of the bird and kept it very succulent while it roasted, plus you got the perfect skin on top and a stock-rich pool below. Pot-roasting is now fashionable once again. A good thing too, because, along with poaching and steaming, it's the best way to cook chicken. You can roast the bird breast side down first, then turn it, but once it's in the oven, it's nice to forget about it and life can be made even easier if the whole meal can come out of the same pot. Apart from convenience, you cash in on all of the bird's flavor, as the pot holds a sauna-like microcosm of chickeness that'll sop into anything that's nestling alongside.

Chicken and pea shoot salad

Pea shoots are the tender growing tips of snowpea plants, and need no cooking. They are commonly sold by Chinese grocers as *dau mui* and are used in salads and stir-fries. You'll need to perk them up in ice-cold water just before using. Other leaves can be used instead, such as watercress, baby spinach, or finely sliced uncooked snowpeas. This quick-to-prepare salad recipe is very adaptable, so use whatever leaves you can find.

1 cooked chicken, preferably poached

3 tablespoons sour cream

3 handfuls pea shoots

6 radishes, sliced

1 cup cherry or baby plum tomatoes, halved

sea salt and freshly ground black pepper

Ginger marinade:

1 garlic clove, crushed

3 tablespoons rice vinegar

juice of 1 lemon

1½ tablespoons sugar

1 whole clove, very finely crushed

2 fresh kaffir lime leaves, very finely chopped (optional)

½ teaspoon chile flakes

1 inch fresh ginger, finely grated, then the juice squeezed from the gratings, solids discarded

Serves 6

Variations:

• To make a different dressing, use 3 tablespoons pureéd tofu with ½ tablespoon tahini paste instead of sour cream.

• Instead of pea shoots, use other herbs, or a package of mixed herb salad.

• Make extra dressing and toss into a salad of steamed rice and fresh cilantro.

1

Remove all the meat from the chicken and pull it into shreds.

2

To make the ginger marinade, put all the ingredients in a large bowl and beat well. Add the chicken and turn to coat well. Chill for at least 1 hour or overnight.

3

Remove the chicken from the marinade. Beat the sour cream into the marinade juices, then add salt and pepper to taste.

4

Carefully fold the chicken with the pea shoots, radishes, and tomatoes, then pile into bowls or onto serving plates. Spoon over the sour cream dressing and serve.

Mango lapsang chicken
and herb salad with honey and sesame dressing

To slice a mango in half you must cut parallel to the elliptical flat side of the stone. It's not as complicated as it sounds. The outward shape mirrors the internal seed—always cut lengthwise with the mango positioned narrow end down. When you hit the seed, slice around it as you cut through. For this recipe choose firm fruit—too ripe and the flesh will disintegrate as you slice.

½ cooked chicken, cut in half

2 tablespoons rice vinegar

1 tablespoon sugar

1 garlic clove

1 small hot chile, very finely chopped

shredded curly endive, fresh rinsed bean sprouts, or baby spinach

4 scallions, trimmed and shredded

2 handfuls cilantro, mint, and basil

1 very large firm mango, peeled, sides sliced off parallel to the seed, then cut into wafer-thin slices

2 tablespoons black (or white) sesame seeds, toasted in a dry skillet

Smoking mixture (optional):

¼ cup Lapsang souchong tea leaves

3 tablespoons brown sugar

3 tablespoons uncooked rice

Honey and Sesame dressing:

5 tablespoons honey

3 tablespoons rice vinegar

½ cup peanut oil

2 teaspoons sesame oil

*Serves 4 as a light lunch,
8 as an appetizer*

1

To smoke the chicken, line the base of a steamer with a double thickness of foil. Spread the smoking mixture ingredients over the foil. Put the chicken in the steaming tray, assemble steamer, and cover with a lid. Place over a gentle heat until the smoke rises and smoke for about 20 minutes. Alternatively, omit the smoking step and use plain cooked chicken.

2

Mix the rice vinegar, sugar, garlic, and chile and stir until the sugar has dissolved.

3

Discard the chicken skin (and smoking ingredients), flake the meat from the bone, and toss with the rice vinegar mixture.

4

To make the dressing, put the honey and vinegar in a food processor and blend. Gradually add the peanut and sesame oils through the feed tube of the processor, until fully amalgamated, as if making mayonnaise. The dressing should be of sauce consistency. Use half for this salad and use the remainder for other dishes.

5

Mix the chicken with the endive, bean sprouts or spinach, then add the scallions, cilantro, mint, and basil. Put neat piles onto plates or into bowls, then served topped with sliced mango, the honey and sesame dressing, and the toasted sesame seeds.

Char-grilled chicken

and pumpkin couscous with honey, mint, and cardamom lemon oil

Don't be put off by the long list of ingredients—though there are many different spices, they are all quite ordinary things by today's standards and you probably have them in your pantry already.

⅔ cup olive oil

20 cardamom pods, crushed

1 large whole lemon,
coarsely chopped

6 chicken breast fillets

1 butternut squash, halved,
seeded, and thickly sliced

1 chicken stock cube

1 lb. couscous

torn leaves from 1 bunch
of mint, plus extra to serve

a bunch of chives, finely
chopped

2 red onions, halved and
finely sliced

2 garlic cloves, crushed

1 teaspoon ground cumin

1 teaspoon ground coriander

½ teaspoon ground cinnamon

a pinch of saffron (optional)

2 teaspoons honey

1 tablespoon pine nuts

sea salt and freshly ground
black pepper

Serves 6

1

Put the oil, cardamom pods, and lemon in a small skillet and heat gently (do not sauté) until the lemon peel is lightly stewed and softened. Let cool.

2

Season the chicken and squash and rub with some of the cardamom lemon oil. Preheat a stove-top grill pan (ridged, if you want black lines) or charcoal grill, add the chicken and squash, and cook for about 2–3 minutes on each side.

3

Dissolve the stock cube in 4 cups boiling water. Put the couscous in a bowl and pour over enough stock to barely cover (don't be tempted to add more stock). Season and let swell. Fluff through with a fork after 5 minutes. Stir in the mint and chives.

4

Heat 1 tablespoon of the oil in a large shallow saucepan, add the onions, garlic, and ground spices and sauté until the onions are soft. Add the saffron, if using, honey, pine nuts, and remaining stock. Season lightly. Add the pumpkin, put the chicken on top, and heat to simmering. Partly cover the pan with a lid, then cook for 10 minutes until the squash is just soft.

5

Divide the couscous between 6 bowls, add the spiced onion, chicken (sliced if you wish) and squash, pour over the hot juices, then serve topped with a few extra mint leaves.

Variations:

• Use cardamom lemon oil to brush meat or vegetables before broiling or roasting.

Prosciutto chicken kiev

with peas, fava beans, mint, and basil

Chicken kiev needs no introduction. We all love it. This one is made with chicken legs, which have far more succulence and flavor than breasts. It's also wrapped in prosciutto instead of breadcrumbs and roasted rather than fried. To save time, you can prepare the chicken the day before.

1¼ cups soft butter

5 garlic cloves, crushed

5 tablespoons finely chopped parsley

2 tablespoons finely chopped basil

6 chicken legs, skinned, foot joint removed, then boned*

12 thin slices prosciutto

2½ cups shelled fresh green peas

2½ cups shelled fresh fava beans

2½ cups yellow wax beans or green beans

1 handful of fresh mint leaves

1 handful of fresh basil leaves

1 bunch of fresh chives

sea salt and freshly ground black pepper

olive oil, for brushing

Serves 6

Note: *To bone the legs, start from the "hip," separating the meat from the bone with the tip of a sharp knife. Follow the bone, keeping the flesh intact until you reach the "knee." Roll back the flesh and carefully scrape the meat from around the cartilage— don't worry about making a few holes. Proceed half way down the next bone, fold back the meat, and cut off the bone. A small "handle" of bone will remain. (Your butcher may do this job for you.)*

1

Mash the butter with the garlic, parsley, basil, salt, and pepper. Stuff into the leg cavities and cover the openings with the loose flap of flesh. Wrap 2 overlapping slices of prosciutto around each leg and stand them upright on in oiled roasting pan. (It can be prepared to this point, wrapped in plastic wrap, refrigerated overnight, then cooked the next day.)

2

Brush the chicken with oil and roast in a preheated oven at 425°F for 25 minutes or until crisp. Pierce with the point of a sharp knife: the juices will run clear when the chicken is done.

3

Simmer the peas and beans in boiling salted water until *al dente*, about 4 minutes. Drain and mix in the herbs.

4

To serve, put one prosciutto chicken kiev in each bowl or plate, surround with the peas, beans, and leaves of mint, basil, and chives. Pour over the caramelized juices from the roasting pan, then serve.

Persian chicken with coconut and almonds

Almonds and pistachios, typical in Persian and Moghul cooking, are prized for their color and flavor. The easiest way to get inside a coconut is to put it inside two plastic bags then slam it on a solid floor. Peel the skin then grate the flesh. The curry improves with time, so try to make it the day before.

6 chicken legs, skinned and cut into thigh and drumstick pieces

½ teaspoon ground cinnamon

½ teaspoon ground cloves

⅓ cup sunflower oil

8 garlic cloves, chopped

2½ inches fresh ginger, chopped

5 tablespoons blanched whole almonds

2 large onions, chopped

5 dried chiles

8 black cardamom pods, bruised

6 teaspoons garam masala*

8 tablespoons plain yogurt

1¾ cups canned coconut milk

2 tablespoons golden raisins

salt

To serve:

finely grated flesh of ½ fresh coconut

2 tablespoons slivered nuts, such as almonds and pistachios

6 small bananas, sliced (optional)

Serves 6

***Note:** Garam masala is sold in gourmet stores and Asian, especially Indian, markets. If unavailable, use half ground cinnamon, half chile powder. The whole chiles and cardamoms are for flavoring— tell your guests not to eat them.*

1

Rub the chicken pieces with the cinnamon, cloves, and a little salt. Heat the oil in a non-stick skillet, add the chicken and sauté on all sides until golden. Transfer to a flameproof casserole. Retain the oil in the skillet.

2

Put the garlic, ginger, almonds, and onions in a food processor and work to a paste, adding a drop of water if necessary.

3

Add the chiles and black cardamom pods to the oil and sauté until the chiles blister. Add the onion mixture and garam masala and sauté until the paste darkens—keep stirring to avoid burning. Strain off excess oil.

4

Slowly stir in the yogurt, 1 tablespoon at a time, then stir in the coconut milk, ½ cup water, and the raisins. Pour around the chicken in the casserole and heat to simmering. Cook, covered, in a preheated oven at 300°F for 1 hour.

5

Serve topped with grated coconut, slivered nuts, and banana, if using.

Clay pot lemon poussin

Lemon chicken with buttery garlic rice is my idea of perfect chicken—and putting everything in one pot is perfection too: no juices are lost and you can scrape the cooking dish clean at the table, down to every last caramelized buttery morsel. Using individual pots also makes serving easy as there's no "dishing up"—everything is already portioned. If you haven't got four small pots, you can cook all the birds and the rice in one large pot, then serve on warm plates.

⅔ cup butter, softened

6 garlic cloves, 4 smashed and 2 crushed

a bunch of parsley, finely chopped

4 unwaxed lemons, juice of 1, the rest cut into wedges

4 poussin (baby chickens or coquelets), preferably free-range

2 tablespoons olive oil

2 cups long grain rice

sea salt and freshly ground black pepper

Serves 4

1

Mix ½ cup of the butter with the 2 crushed garlic cloves and chopped parsley. Season well.

2

Put 1 wedge of lemon, 1 smashed garlic clove and 1 heaped teaspoon of the butter mixture inside each chicken and tie the legs together with string. Rub with salt and pepper.

3

Heat the remaining butter with the oil in a large skillet and brown the birds on all sides. Put the birds in the pots.

4

Mix the remaining garlic parsley butter with the rice and distribute around each chicken. Drizzle the lemon juice over each bird and tuck in the remaining lemon wedges. Add ½ cup water to each pot, cover, and cook in a preheated oven at 425°F for 45—50 minutes. If you want greenery, serve a bowl of green beans for everyone to help themselves.

Variations:

• To make Moroccan lemon chicken, instead of parsley, mix saffron with the butter, add golden raisins and toasted pine nuts to the rice and bake, with preserved lemons instead of fresh. You could also rub the chicken before sautéing with a little paprika, ground cumin, cinnamon, and ginger.

Chicken and mushroom pie

This classic pie is made extra-good with morels, which give it an added wood-smoked flavor. Dried morels are always available, and picked and dried in their prime, can be much better than many so-called "fresh" ones.

1½ lb. fresh ready-made shortcrust pastry dough

½ cup butter, softened

1 whole cooked chicken, about 5 lb.

1 onion, quartered

2 garlic cloves

1 fresh bouquet garni of bay leaves, parsley and leek

3 blades mace or a pinch of powdered mace

3 cups good chicken stock

18 fresh morels, brushed clean, or 2 oz. dried (soaked in water until soft) or a mixture of wild mushrooms, including morels

1½ tablespoons all-purpose flour

½ cup heavy cream

1 egg, lightly beaten

sea salt and freshly ground black pepper

1 fresh chanterelle, to serve (optional)

Serves 6

1

Roll out the pastry dough to ⅛ inch thick. Spread two-thirds of the butter over half of the pastry and fold the other half over the top. Repeat and fold twice more. Press together and chill for 30 minutes (this will make the pastry flaky).

2

Flake the chicken into chunks. Discard the skin and bones.

3

Put the onion, garlic, bouquet garni, mace, and stock in a saucepan, bring to a boil, then simmer for 10 minutes. Boil until reduced by three-quarters. Strain and discard the solids.

4

Heat the remaining butter in a skillet, add the morels and sauté for 1–2 minutes and remove. Add the flour and cook to a paste. Stir in the reduced stock and simmer to a thick sauce. Add the cream and the fried mushrooms and let boil for about 2 minutes. Taste and adjust the seasoning.

5

Roll out half the pastry and use to line an 7-inch greased pie dish. Roll out the remaining pastry and slice into ribbons about 2 inches wide. Weave together. Fill the pie shell with the chicken and mushrooms. Pour in the cream sauce. Brush the top edge of the case with beaten egg and arrange the pastry weave on top. Trim the edges and then press together. Brush with beaten egg and bake in a preheated oven at 350°F for 1 hour. Serve, topped with the fresh chanterelle, if using.

Honeyed duck

with baby chard, cilantro, and mustard seed mayo in ciabatta

Duck breast lends itself to fast cooking—a few minutes in a searingly hot skillet is all it needs. It's at its best when the skin is caramelized to a sticky crisp, yet the meat remains rare, pink, and very tender. In fact, cook the breasts as you would do for a steak. These great-tasting duck and salad pocket sandwiches could also be served in pitta bread or between toast, or just as a salad dressed with mustard seed mayo for a light lunch.

1 large duck breast

1 teaspoon five-spice powder

1 tablespoon honey

1 tablespoon light soy sauce

1 teaspoon cumin seeds

2 teaspoons sesame seeds, toasted in a dry skillet

½ tablespoon whole-grain mustard

2 tablespoons mayonnaise

a handful of baby chard leaves or other robust salad leaves

a handful of mizuna or frisée leaves

a handful of cilantro stems, coarsely chopped

a handful of scallions, sliced lengthwise into strips

ciabatta rolls, halved and hollowed, pitta breads, or buttered toast

sea salt and freshly ground black pepper

Serves 4–6

1

Score fine cuts across the skin of the duck and rub with salt and five-spice powder. Pour over the honey and soy sauce, rub in, and marinate for 1–2 hours in the refrigerator.

2

Put the duck breast, skin side down, in a preheated heavy-bottom skillet, and char-grill for 4 minutes. Turn it over and cook for a further 4–5 minutes. The skin will look charred but won't taste burnt: the flesh should be pink. Let it rest for 10 minutes, then cut crosswise into thin slices.

3

Mix the cumin seeds, sesame seeds, and mustard with the mayonnaise. Coat the inside of the breads with the mixture and stuff with the remaining ingredients.

Kumquat duck with chile citrus sauce

Kumquats or cumquats are sharply tangy and look like cocktail oranges (if there could be such a thing). It's the skin that has the flavor, don't even think of trying to peel one (you'll end up with nothing)—they're the snowpea of the citrus world and are best cooked. If you roast whole ducks, the leg meat can be shredded and used to make spring rolls and any remaining citrus sauce can be used as a dipping sauce.

3 large duck breasts

1 tablespoon honey

¼ cup tablespoons soy sauce

salt

Chile citrus sauce:

12 kumquats, quartered

1 inch fresh ginger, peeled and grated

2 shallots, finely sliced lengthwise

2 garlic cloves, chopped

4 tablespoons sugar

1 tablespoon fish sauce

2 tablespoons rice vinegar

juice of 4 oranges, preferably blood oranges

juice of 2 limes

2 small red mild chiles, quartered and seeded

1 tablespoon cornstarch, blended with 2 tablespoons water

To serve:

2 long red mild chiles, seeded and sliced into fine long shreds

watercress (optional)

scallions (optional)

Serves 6

1

Using a sharp knife, finely score the duck skin. Mix the honey with the soy sauce. Rub the breasts with a little salt, then with the soy mixture, cover, and chill for at least 30 minutes or overnight.

2

To make the sauce, put the kumquats, ginger, shallots, garlic, sugar, and 1 cup water in a saucepan and fast simmer for about 10 minutes until reduced by half. Stir in the other ingredients, except the cornstarch paste, simmer gently for 5 minutes, then strain the syrup into a clean pan. Return the kumquat peel to the syrup (discard the remaining contents of the strainer). Add the blended cornstarch and boil the syrup for 1 minute to thicken.

3

Roast the duck breasts in a preheated oven at 425°F for 15 minutes or until golden. Let rest for 5 minutes, then slice thickly. Reheat the sauce. Slice the duck, pile into bowls, coat with the sauce, add the sliced chiles, watercress, and scallions, if using, and serve with plain boiled rice.

Variations:

• Serve the sauce with crispy reef fish. Score the fish on both flanks with parallel cuts and rub with seasoning. Heat vegetable oil in a deep saucepan and slide in the fish—head first. Fry for 5–8 minutes, then serve dressed with the chile citrus sauce and sliced shallots.

• Use the duck to make spring rolls, adding cucumber, scallions, sesame oil, soy sauce, and bean sprouts. Roll up in spring roll wrappers and deep-fry in corn oil. Serve with the sauce.

Root and honey duck hot pot

For this dish, I make my own duck stock out of the pre-roasted duck carcass but you can use four duck pieces and bought chicken stock instead. Add potatoes and squash if you want a more substantial meal, or just serve with crusty bread. Double-roasting the duck releases more fat and tenderizes the flesh, a bit like duck confit – roast it just once if you prefer it pink.

1 duck or 6 duck legs

½ teaspoon ground mace or ¼ teaspoon freshly grated nutmeg

1½ tablespoons honey

2 tablespoons olive oil

1 leek, white and pale green part only, chopped

2 celery stalks (with leaves) or Chinese celery, stalks chopped, leaves reserved

2 garlic cloves, finely chopped

1 teaspoon coriander seeds

½ teaspoon cumin seeds, toasted in a hot dry skillet

4 cups well-seasoned chicken stock

1½ lb. mixed root vegetables, such as parsnips or Hamburg parsley root, small turnips and salsify, all peeled and with any large roots thickly sliced

a good squeeze of fresh lemon juice

sea salt and freshly ground black pepper

Serves 6

1
If using a whole duck, prick it all over with a sharp knife (plus a few extra stabs around the flanks and fatty parts), rub with salt, pepper, and mace or nutmeg. Put on a rack over a roasting pan, then rub with 1 tablespoon of the honey. Roast in a preheated oven at 375°F for 1 hour.

2
Loosely cover with foil, let cool, then cut into quarters. Discard the ribs and backbone or use to make a stock. At this point the duck can be refrigerated for up to 3 days if you wish: it will become wrinkled and pallid, but when re-roasted will turn mahogany brown, plump, and crisp.

3
If using duck portions, slash the skin and fat with a sharp knife and prepare as above. Put in a roasting pan and cook in a preheated oven at 375°F for 40 minutes. Let cool as above.

4
Heat the oil in a large skillet, add the chopped leek, celery stalks, garlic, cilantro, and cumin seeds and gently sauté until the vegetables have softened but not browned. Add the stock and bring to a boil, stir in the remaining honey, then add the roots and gently simmer for 25 minutes. Add the lemon juice, then taste and adjust the seasoning.

5
Meanwhile, re-roast the duck portions for 15 minutes at 425°F until crisp and brown. Chop or flake the meat and divide between 6 Chinese-style bowls. Add the soup and vegetables and top with the celery leaves.

Christmas turkey for two

with clove stuffing and sprouts

You want turkey on the big day but you don't want the big bird? Easy. You can get the whole Christmas dinner experience with just a drumstick, stuffed then wrapped in bacon. Drumsticks may be considered the poor man's cut, yet the dark meat has all the flavour and the bacon wrapping keeps it moist.

⅔ cup milk

15 whole cloves, lightly crushed

2 bay leaves

1 onion, halved

10 thick slices white bread, crusts removed, processed to crumbs

1 turkey drumstick

6 slices bacon,

1 tablespoon butter

3 cups (about 24) Brussels sprouts (or as many as you wish), outer leaves removed if necessary

sea salt and freshly ground black pepper

Serves 2

1

Put the milk, cloves, bay leaves, and onion in a small saucepan, bring to a boil, then simmer gently for about 10 minutes. Let cool, then strain into another pan. Finely chop half the cooked onion and add to the milk pan. Discard the rest of the onion, the cloves, and bay leaves.

2

Add the breadcrumbs to the pan, season, and simmer gently, stirring, for about 5 minutes until you have a thick paste.

3

Using a sharp, narrow-bladed knife, bone the turkey drumstick, starting at the thigh end. Release the meat from the bone all the way down inside the leg. Pull out the bone. If you want a piece of bone showing (as shown in the photograph), chop off the end of the bone with a heavy cleaver and reposition it just inside the leg cavity. Stuff the leg with the clove stuffing, secure the opening with toothpicks, and rub with seasoning. Wrap the bacon in overlapping spiralling layers around the leg and put in a roasting pan. Smother with the butter and roast in a preheated oven at 400°F for 50 minutes (cover with foil if the bacon starts to brown too much).

4

Cook the sprouts in boiling salted water for about 6 minutes or until tender (*al dente* is not quite cooked enough for my liking). Drain and toss in some of the turkey pan juices and serve with roast potatoes and gravy. The leg can be sliced right through into rounds—perfect portion control.

Pot-roasted game bird

with apple, cabbage, juniper, and cream

A cross between a roast and a stew, you can put this dish in the oven, set the timer, and forget about it. This method keeps the bird moist and tender so the meat will fall from the bones, just the way you want it.

1 game bird, such as pheasant
or guinea fowl, or a chicken, well seasoned

3 tablespoons olive oil

¼ cup butter

8 small pickling onions or shallots

2 garlic cloves, crushed

8 juniper berries, crushed

¾ cup hard cider

⅔ cup good chicken stock

8 baby apples or 4 large, cored and quartered

greens such as the outer leaves of a
Savoy cabbage, red brussels tops, or
other cabbage, separated into leaves,
thick ribs removed

⅔ cup heavy cream

sea salt and freshly ground black pepper

Serves 4

1

Heat the oil and half the butter in a large skillet, add the bird, and brown it on all sides. Transfer to a deep snug-fitting flameproof casserole.

2

Wipe the skillet, then add the remaining butter, onions, garlic, and juniper, and sauté gently for 2 minutes. Pour in the cider and stock. Simmer for 5 minutes. Add the apples and transfer to the casserole dish.

3

Heat to simmering, cover with a lid, then transfer to a preheated oven and cook at 350°F for 45 minutes.

4

Blanch the cabbage leaves in boiling water for 3 minutes, then tuck the leaves around the bird, pour over the cream, return to the oven, and cook for a further 15 minutes.

5

Cut the bird into pieces and serve with the apple, cabbage, and juices. Other good accompaniments are sautéed potatoes or potatoes mashed with parsnips, then flavored with truffle oil.

Squab and peach tagine

Squab are farm-reared pigeons. Their meat is succulent and tender, far superior to wood pigeon. Consequently they're a little expensive and can be difficult to find. Duck breast, guinea fowl pieces, or quail will work just as well, but remember to roast the larger birds for longer, about 20 minutes per pound, while the quail will only need about 8 minutes.

3 squab (French pigeon)

1 teaspoon ground ginger

½ teaspoon ground cinnamon

1 teaspoon ground mace (optional)

olive oil, for brushing and sautéing

4 large onions, finely sliced

4 bay leaves

a pinch of saffron (optional)

14 oz. couscous

chicken stock (see method)

4 garlic cloves, crushed

2 teaspoons paprika

1 teaspoon cumin

1 teaspoon coriander seeds

6 cardamom pods

1½ tablespoons pine nuts

3 tablespoons raisins

4 firm peaches, sliced into wedges

sea salt and freshly ground black pepper

Serves 6

1

Rub the squab with salt, pepper, ginger, cinnamon, and mace, if using. Brush with olive oil and put on a baking tray. Roast in a preheated oven at 400°F for 15 minutes. Remove from the oven and let cool.

2

Slice the breast meat and legs from each bird and set side. Chop up the wings and carcass and put in a saucepan with 5 cups water. Add half a sliced onion, the bay leaves, salt, and pepper. Bring to a boil, then simmer until reduced to about half volume. Strain and discard all the bones. Add the saffron to the strained stock and infuse for about 10 minutes.

3

Put the couscous in a bowl and pour in the stock until the grains are just covered. Let stand for 5 minutes, then fluff up with a fork. Keep it warm.

4

Heat 3 tablespoons olive oil in a skillet, add the remaining onion and the garlic, and sauté until soft and lightly caramelized. Add all the spices, pine nuts, and raisins and sauté for a few minutes more.

5

Spoon the mixture into a shallow saucepan or skillet with a lid. Pour over the remaining stock. Put a layer of sliced peaches on the top, then a layer of squab pieces. Cover and simmer over a low heat for about 10 minutes.

6

Serve on heated dinner plates with separate bowls of saffron couscous.

meat

There are those days when a wine-rich beef stew, a braised shoulder of lamb or roast crackling pork is the only food that will hit the mark. It's then, when it's right miserable out, you gravitate to all things comfy, like the sofa, TV, and slow-cooked food—and that means meat. In winter, little beats a pot of clove-braised cabbage with pan-crusted sausages or a melting beef pie filled with rich onion gravy. Spring and summer are times to enjoy faster cooked, tender cuts of lamb, rare steak, or a ham, with herb olive oil or creamy buttered sauces, garden pods, and leaves. Great tasting meat needs little to show it off, but make sure you buy the right cut to suit the way you're going to cook it. As a guide, the less expensive cuts of meat are coarse-grained, such as beef bottom round, brisket, and chuck. They are suited to slow braising, whereas the leaner, more expensive cuts, such as tenderloin and rib-eye are best cooked fast and kept rare—pork though should always be cooked right through.

And remember, the best beef, pork, and lamb come from happy animals. They've been allowed to grow up as naturally as possible, to graze, root, and forage in fields and fresh air, interact with each other, build muscle without in-feed antibiotics and hormones; and have been transported and slaughtered as humanely as possible. So next time you choose your roast, ask your butcher about the meat you're buying. Happy meat may cost a little more, but when you think of the life of the animal and the results, it's really worth it.

Beef stew with chestnuts

Blade of beef (from the shoulder) is the best cut of meat to use: it is marbled with fat and connective tissue and especially suited to long, slow-cooking. The meat is lubricated as it cooks, becoming moist and tender. Use fresh chestnuts or, for ease, use the peeled, part-cooked vacumn-packed variety.

3 lb. blade or
stewing steak,
cut into 4 pieces

3½ tablespoons
beef dripping or
olive oil

1 large onion,
finely chopped

2 garlic cloves,
crushed

2 bay leaves

1 star anise
(optional)

2 carrots,
finely chopped

2 celery stalks,
finely chopped

1 tablespoon
tomato purée

1½ bottles red wine

18 chestnuts

1 teaspoon sugar

salt and freshly
ground black
pepper

Serves 6–8

1

Rub the meat with salt and plenty of pepper. Heat a heavy, flameproof casserole until hot, add 2 tablespoons dripping or oil, and add the meat. Leave without moving until well browned and caramelized, about 2 minutes. Turn over and continue browning until all sides are done. Remove from the casserole.

2

Add 1 tablespoon dripping or oil, add the onion, garlic, bay leaves, star anise, if using, carrots, and celery and sauté until browned. Add salt and pepper, stir in the tomato purée, and cook for 1 minute. Add the wine and 1¼ cups water, bring to a boil, then simmer until reduced by half.

3

Put the meat back into the casserole with the vegetable-wine mixture, cover, and let braise gently in a preheated oven at 300°F for 3 hours.

4

If using fresh chestnuts, part-slice the chestnut skins open on their curved side, then boil for 5 minutes. Strain, cool, then peel and remove the brown pith. Cut in half. Heat the remaining dripping or oil in a frying pan, add the sugar and chestnuts, and sauté until caramelized, about 3 minutes. Add to the casserole, then return to the oven to braise for a further 40 minutes. Serve with buttery mashed potatoes flavored with mustard or horseradish.

Pub beef and onion pies

The best beef and onion pies are found in British pubs. I like this easy hot water crust pastry, but you can use bought shortcrust or puff pastry instead.

¼ cup butter, for frying

2 lb. braising steak, cubed

5 onions, 1 sliced lengthwise, 4 halved and finely sliced

2 dried bay leaves, ground or very finely crumbled

2 tablespoons all-purpose flour

2 teaspoons Worcestershire sauce

2 teaspoons tomato purée

1 teaspoon anchovy sauce

1 tablespoon mushroom sauce

2 cups Guinness Stout

2 teaspoons sugar

1 tablespoon wine vinegar

salt and freshly cracked black pepper

hot English mustard, to serve (optional)

Hot water crust pastry:

3 cups all-purpose flour

a large pinch of salt

¾ cup lard

⅔ cup milk

1 egg yolk, to glaze

Serves 6

6 small rectangular pie dishes

1

Heat 1 tablespoon of the butter in a deep skillet. Season the meat and brown in batches. Remove and keep warm.

2

Heat the remaining butter in the skillet, add the finely sliced onions and bay leaves, and sauté until lightly browned. Season, stir in the flour, adding extra butter if necessary, and sauté until the onion mixture is a rich brown.

3

Stir in the Worcestershire sauce, tomato purée, anchovy sauce, mushroom sauce, Guinness Stout, sugar, and vinegar, and let bubble for 5 minutes. Stir in 1¼ cups water, cover, and simmer gently for 1½ hours. Spoon into the pie dishes.

4

To make the pastry, sift the flour and salt into a bowl. Put the lard, milk and ⅔ cup water in a saucepan and bring to a boil. Stir into the flour, let cool, then knead gently but firmly. Use immediately—do not refrigerate.

5

Roll out the pastry to ⅛ inch thick. Cut 6 rectangles to fit the tops of the pie dishes and press an onion slice into each. Cut small strips from the remaining pastry and use to line the rim of each dish, pressing firmly. Place a pastry lid on top and, using your fingers or tip of a knife, press the edges onto the pastry-lined rim to seal. Make a small hole in the top of each pie to let the steam escape, brush with egg yolk, and bake in a preheated oven at 400°F for 30 minutes.

6

Serve with mustard, if using, and boiled potatoes or mashed potatoes.

Lamb burgers

with char-grilled eggplant, hummus, seed salt, and mint

Homemade burgers are vastly superior to store-bought ones, and so easy to make that we should all make them more often—everyone loves a burger. The seed salt is delicious—store the extra and use it in lots of other ways.

2 tablespoons olive oil, plus extra for brushing

1 onion, finely chopped

2 cloves garlic, crushed

1 small chile, very finely chopped (optional)

1 lb. ground lamb

a handful of mint leaves, chopped, plus extra leaves to serve

1 eggplant, sliced lengthwise

sea salt and freshly ground black pepper

6 oz. hummus, to serve

Seed salt:

1 tablespoon cumin seeds

1 tablespoon sesame seeds

1 tablespoon sea salt

Makes 6 burgers

1

To make the seed salt, toast the cumin seeds and sesame seeds in a dry skillet until the sesame seeds are a light golden brown (watch them, and turn them regularly—they'll burn if left alone). Mix in a bowl with the salt.

2

Heat half the olive oil in the skillet, add the onion, garlic, chile, 2 teaspoons seed salt, and black pepper, and sauté until the onion is soft and transparent.

3

Put the ground lamb in a bowl with the chopped mint, the onion mixture, salt, and freshly ground black pepper. Mix well. Shape into burgers, brush with oil, and cook under a hot broiler or in a preheated stove-top grill pan until crisp and brown outside and pink in the middle. Remove and drain on paper towels.

4

Brush the eggplant slices on both sides with the remaining oil and season with salt and pepper. Char-grill on both sides until seared with black lines and softened.

5

Serve the lamb burgers topped with a spoonful of hummus and a fold of eggplant, sprinkled with a little seed salt and a few mint leaves.

Variations:

• To make *baba ganoush*, mash the eggplant with lemon juice, tahini, olive oil, crushed garlic, seed salt, and chopped mint—serve with minted lamb meat balls (use burger mixture).

Rosemary and olive lamb

with roasted garlic lima beans

I've used rack of lamb but if you are cooking for more than four people, you should use leg or shoulder as in the variation. If you've just decided you want to cook this today, use canned lima beans instead (omit step 1)—cannellini beans are equally good.

4 cups dried lima beans, soaked overnight in cold water to cover, then drained

1 onion

2 whole heads of garlic, separated into cloves (skin on)

½ bouillon cube (chicken or lamb), crumbled

1 fresh bouquet garni (fresh bay leaves, sprigs of thyme, parsley, and rosemary)

1 rack of lamb (total 12 ribs), trimmed of excess fat

leaves from 1 small bunch of rosemary, chopped

8 black olives, pitted and chopped

2 tablespoons olive oil

sea salt and freshly ground black pepper

Serves 4–6

1

Put the beans, onion, 4 peeled garlic cloves, bouillon cube, and bouquet garni in a saucepan, cover with cold water, and bring to the a boil. Skim off any foam, lower the heat after 5 minutes, and gently simmer for 1 hour or until the beans are tender (season only during the last 10 minutes of cooking). Let cool in the juices. Discard the onion, garlic, and bouquet garni.

2

Rub the lamb with salt and pepper and coat the fat side with the chopped rosemary and chopped olives, pressing on well. Put the rack of lamb in a roasting pan, tuck the unpeeled garlic cloves underneath, and spoon the oil over the top. Roast in a preheated oven at 400°F for 20–25 minutes until the meat is medium-rare, or until cooked to your liking.

3

Meanwhile, reheat the beans in their cooking liquid. When the lamb is cooked, remove from the pan, cover with foil, and let rest for 5 minutes. Pop the garlic cloves out of their papery skins, strain the beans, and mix with the roasted garlic cloves in the pan. Transfer to a warmed serving dish. Slice the lamb and place on top of the roasted garlic lima beans.

Variations:

• If using a leg of lamb, roast for 20–25 minutes per pound, adding the garlic to the roasting pan 25 minutes before the end of the cooking time. Let the meat rest for 10 minutes before carving. If you need to keep everything warm, the cooked beans and skinned garlic cloves can be spooned around the lamb in the pan.

• If using shoulder of lamb, open-roast until brown, then put in a casserole and braise with the beans until meltingly tender.

Lamb shanks

with squash ratatouille

Lamb shank is the upper foreleg of the animal. Allow for 3 hours of slow braising—this one can't be rushed. In fact the shanks taste better if cooked the day before (until stage 3) and left to saturate and cool in their juices; the final result is meat that is meltingly tender and falls from the bone.

6 lamb shanks, trimmed

5 garlic cloves, cut into slivers

4 tablespoons olive oil, for cooking, plus extra, for brushing

2 large onions, finely chopped

2 large carrots, finely chopped

3 sticks celery, finely chopped

2 tablespoons tomato paste

3 bay leaves

3 strips orange peel

1¼ cups white wine

3 red peppers, seeded and sliced, or 3 Italian sun-dried red peppers*

1 butternut or acorn squash, halved lengthwise, peeled, seeded, and sliced

1 tablespoon capers

1¼ cups black olives, pitted if preferred

small bunch basil, leaves only

sea salt and freshly ground black pepper

Serves 6

From Italian gourmet stores.

1

Season the lamb and stab them all over with a knife. Insert the garlic slivers into the incisions. Heat 2 tablespoons of the oil in a large, heavy-bottom skillet. Brush each shank with olive oil, add to the skillet in batches, and sauté until brown on all sides. Remove and set aside. Add a little more oil to the skillet and heat gently.

2

Add the onion, carrot, and celery and sauté until browned. Mix in the tomato paste, bay leaves, orange peel, and seasoning. Cook for 2 minutes. Add the wine and 1¼ cups water, bring to a boil, then simmer until reduced by half. Transfer to a small, deep roasting pan.

3

Add the lamb shanks to the pan, cover tightly with foil, and cook in a preheated oven at 300°F for about 2 hours.

4

Heat the remaining oil in the skillet. Brush the peppers with olive oil and season with salt and freshly ground black pepper. Add to the skillet and cook until lightly browned on both sides. Add to the lamb shanks, then add the squash, capers, olives, and a little extra water if necessary. Continue braising for 1 hour or until the squash is tender.

5

Remove from the oven, then top with the basil leaves and serve with creamy mashed potatoes or crusty bread.

Pork chops with peppered wild mushroom gravy

No-nonsense pork chops with a rich mushroom gravy and a bowl of mashed potatoes to mop it up—soul-warming stuff. Any mixture of "wild" funghi will do, including chanterelles and porcini, but you can also achieve good results with large open-cap mushrooms or smaller ones, just larger than buttons (slip in few slices of dried porcini to get the "wild" flavor).

¼ cup butter

3 tablespoons olive oil

4 garlic cloves, finely chopped

2 onions, chopped

3 bay leaves

4 tablespoons sherry vinegar

¾ cup sherry or Madeira

1 oz. dried porcini, soaked in ⅔ cup hot water until soft

3¼ cups chicken stock

6 pork chops, trimmed of excess fat

1 lb. mixed "wild" and cultivated mushrooms

sea salt and freshly ground black pepper

creamy mashed potatoes, to serve (optional)

Serves 6

1

Heat half the butter and half the olive oil in a skillet, add half the garlic, the onion, bay leaves, and seasoning, and sauté until the onion becomes translucent. Add the sherry vinegar and reduce until almost dry, then add the sherry, the porcini, their soaking water, and the stock to the skillet and simmer for 20 minutes or until reduced by half. Strain into a clean, wide saucepan and discard all the residue, including the porcini.

2

Heat a ridged stove-top grill pan or heavy-bottom skillet until smoking hot. Rub the pork with salt, pepper, and a little of the olive oil and char-grill for 4 minutes on each side.

3

Cut medium-sized mushrooms in half, trim off any woody stem tips, and slice any large-cap mushrooms. Heat the remaining oil and butter in the skillet, add the mushrooms and the remaining garlic, and sauté for 2 minutes or until tinged golden brown. Season, then add to the pan of gravy and reheat.

4

Serve the chops, mushroom gravy, and mashed potatoes, if using, on preheated plates and sprinkle generously with black pepper.

Anise braised pork

with Chinese mustard cabbage

Pork has a tendency to dry out when roasted, so braising it—as they do in Peking—semi-immersed in honey-sweetened soy sauce keeps it succulent and, of course, steeps the meat with plenty of Chinese flavor. Don't worry about the quantity of soy sauce—it's for poaching, not eating, and you can freeze it to use again.

2 lb. boned pork leg

2 teaspoons five-spice powder

3 tablespoons peanut oil

1 bottle soy sauce (1¾ cups)

6 small pink shallots, or 1–2 large

2 inches fresh ginger, sliced

3 garlic cloves, sliced

2 small fresh whole red chiles

4 tablespoons mirin (rice wine)

1 tablespoon honey

4 whole star anise

1 Chinese mustard cabbage (*dai gai choi*) or other Chinese greens

sea salt

Serves 6

1

Score the pork rind with diagonal cuts. Put in a colander and pour over a pitcher of boiling water. Pat dry with paper towels. Rub a little salt and five-spice powder into the scored skin. Heat 2 tablespoons of the oil in a skillet, add the pork, skin side down, and sauté until lightly scorched. Add 3 tablespoons soy sauce and reduce until caramelized. Transfer the pork to a casserole or sand pot.

2

Heat the remaining oil in the skillet, add the shallots, ginger, garlic, and chiles, and sauté until browned. Add the mirin, honey, star anise, the remaining soy sauce, and 2¾ cups water. Stir to dissolve the honey. Transfer to the casserole.

3

Bring to a boil, cover, turn the heat to low, and simmer gently for 2–2½ hours until meltingly tender. Put the mustard cabbage leaves around the pork and braise for 5 minutes more.

4

Slice the pork and serve with the cabbage and a few spoonfuls of the casserole juices.

Pecan pork with apple and maple syrup

Boneless loin of pork is perfect for stuffing. You'll need string and bamboo skewers to hold the stuffing in place. Remove the string before serving, but leave the skewers in the meat to hold each piece together.

1 loin of pork (about 3lb.), trimmed but with skin included

½ teaspoon ground allspice

3 tablespoons olive oil

5 tablespoons maple syrup

2 tablespoons butter

6 apples, cored and quartered

salt and freshly ground black pepper

Pecan stuffing:

1½ cups shelled pecans

1 onion, chopped

2 garlic cloves, crushed

leaves from 1 bunch of flat leaf parsley

1 bunch of sage, stems discarded

2 cups fresh breadcrumbs

2 cloves, ground

1 egg, lightly beaten

salt and freshly ground black pepper

Serves 6

1

To make the stuffing, work the nuts in a food processor until finely chopped but not ground. Transfer to a large bowl. Add the onion, garlic, and herbs to the processor and chop finely.

2

Heat 2 tablespoons olive oil in a skillet, add the onion mixture and cook gently until softened. Stir into the pecan mixture, then stir in the ground cloves, salt, pepper, and egg. Open up the natural cavity in the joint and stuff with the pecan stuffing. Close up and tie the length of the loin with string.

3

Place the meat in a roasting pan. Using a craft knife or very sharp kitchen knife, score the skin and fat crosswise with fine parallel slashes. After scoring, place the fat on top of the roast, then secure at regular intervals with skewers. Rub with plenty of salt, pepper, allspice, and the remaining oil. Roast in a preheated oven at 425°F for 30 minutes. Pour over half the maple syrup, lower the heat to 375°F, then roast for a further 45 minutes.

4

Heat the butter in a skillet, add the apple quarters and sauté until lightly browned. Pour in the remaining maple syrup and cook for about 2 minutes until lightly caramelized. Arrange around the pork for the last 10 minutes of cooking. Remove from the oven and set aside, loosely covered with foil, for 10 minutes before carving. To serve, slice the pork as skewered pieces and serve with mashed celery root or mashed parsnips.

Ham and peas

Many meals can be made from a single ham hock—the flakes of succulent meat and the aromatic saturated stock can be used separately or together to make robust, yet elegant, fare. This is real home cooking, but if you don't want to cook your own ham for the salad variation, use store-bought ham.

1 unsmoked ham hock, about 4 lb.

2 bay leaves

stems of flat-leaf parsley

1 teaspoon dried oregano

2 garlic cloves

1 onion, halved

1 teaspoon freshly grated nutmeg

1 tablespoon peppercorns

3 cups shelled green peas

a handful of cooked and skinned fava beans (optional)

leaves from 1 bunch of mint, torn

sea salt

Roasting mix:

1 tablespoon olive oil

1 tablespoon honey

3 teaspoons sea salt

3 whole cloves, ground

freshly ground black pepper

Serves 6

1

Put the ham hock into a deep saucepan and just cover with cold water. Add salt and bring to a boil on top of the stove. Skim off the foam and then add the bay leaves, parsley, oregano, garlic, onion, nutmeg, and peppercorns. Cover and simmer gently for 1 hour.

2

Lift the ham from the saucepan and strain the stock. Slash the skin and rub with olive oil, salt, honey, ground cloves, and pepper. Put in a roasting pan and cook in a preheated oven at 425°F for 45 minutes. If it browns too quickly turn the heat down to 400°F.

3

Put the peas and fava beans, if using, in the roasting pan, fill ½ inch deep with ham stock, and cook for 5 minutes. Remove from the oven.

4

Slice the ham and serve hot, with the peas, beans, and mint.

Variation:

• This recipe is also good served cold as a pea and ham salad with a parsley and mustard dressing. Beat 2 teaspoons Dijon mustard in a bowl with 2 tablespoons cider vinegar and 3 tablespoons olive oil. Beat in a pinch of sugar, a handful of chopped parsley, some chopped green peppercorns, and 1 crushed garlic clove.
To serve, toss the peas with a chopped shallot, torn mint leaves, and olive oil. Add sliced ham and pour over the dressing.

Allspice cabbage
with shallots and sausages

You can use any type of sausage here: regular, herb, game, Italian, Toulouse, or Cajun—the choice is yours. Braised red cabbage is so versatile, it can be left for ages in the oven: it will wait for you rather than you for it. No wonder it's a classic. If everyone is late for supper, just put the cooked sausages in the casserole with the cabbage and keep everything on a low heat until you're ready to eat.

1 red cabbage, halved, cored, and cut into chunks (leaves separated)

4 large banana shallots or 8 shallots, peeled

1 garlic clove, crushed

½ teaspoon crushed cloves

½ teaspoon ground cinnamon

½ teaspoon ground allspice

½ teaspoon freshly grated nutmeg

1½ tablespoons brown sugar

2 tablespoons apple or cranberry jelly

3 tablespoons red wine vinegar

2 tablespoons butter, softened

salt and freshly ground black pepper

12 sausages of your choice, such as regular, herb, game, Itailain, or Toulouse

Serves 6

1

Put all the ingredients except the sausages in a heavy casserole, add 3 tablespoons water and mix well.

2

Cover with a lid and braise in a preheated oven at 300°F for 2 hours. Stir twice during the cooking time so the cabbage and shallots receive their fair share of spice and buttery juices.

3

Broil or sauté the sausages until cooked and well browned all over. If the cabbage is not quite ready, put the sausages on top of the cabbage in the casserole to keep hot. If using banana shallots, remove them from the casserole and cut in half lengthwise before serving. Serve with a generous helping of mashed potato with mustard.

Variations:

• Add golden raisins or prunes, chopped chile, and paprika and serve with roast honeyed duck (page 108) or duck confit.

• Add sliced apples and serve with roasted pork or broiled goat cheese.

As far as I'm concerned a dessert can be eaten at any time of the day. A tart or pastry for breakfast or with a mid-morning coffee can be just the thing you crave to whip up some energy; ice cream on a sweltering afternoon cools, soothes, and relaxes; and a slice of cake or chocolate shortbread with your afternoon cuppa is just the boost you need at the end of the day. Then there's dinner-time dessert, and for some, like your friends who have a sweet tooth, it's the best bit of the meal. That makes at least four desserts you can fit, if somewhat tightly, into your day.

When you've got your friends round for dinner, the last place you should be is in the kitchen. Dessert should have been sorted out well before they descend. They're not there to get all impressed at how clever you are—well, just a little maybe. Anyhow, from my experience if you leave the table for too long, they'll come and find you in the kitchen and start chatting and distracting you from anything you might have planned to be doing. So make sure you've made the dessert well in advance and preferably something that can be served cold or only needs a few minutes in the oven. Something that is simple will look chic because it is so simple. For instance, I think pears are best kept whole or almost whole—you can never chop up a pear, rearrange it and make it look better. Somehow you've just lost its perfect shape. This is why poached pears look so perfect and why I've used them simply halved with stems still attached in my pear tart recipe. The same applies to berries, figs, peaches, and many others. This simplicity is important in all desserts, even those that use the fruit as a flavoring, a filling, or a sauce. If the ingredients are good then you don't need to create elaborate desserts. What a stroke of luck—it makes dessert courses so easy.

desserts

Raspberry ripple

Store-bought ripple is not what it used to be. This one is the real thing and looks the part, with pure vanilla ice cream, streaked with painterly lines of fresh raspberry purée. A classic combination.

2¾ cups milk

1 vanilla bean, split lengthwise

1¼ cups sugar

7 egg yolks

2¾ cups heavy cream, whipped to soft peak stage

Ripple:

8 oz. raspberries, plus extra to serve

5 tablespoons sugar

1 tablespoon lemon juice

Serves 4–6

1

Put the milk and vanilla bean in a saucepan. Bring to a boil, remove from the heat, and let cool for 30 minutes. Discard the vanilla bean.

2

Beat the sugar and egg yolks in a bowl, then pour in the vanilla milk. Put into a saucepan and heat gently, stirring continuously, until you have a thin custard (too much heat and the custard will curdle and separate). Cool, then chill. Fold the whipped cream into the cold custard, pour into a covered container, then freeze.

3

Put the raspberries, sugar, lemon juice, and 1 tablespoon water into a saucepan, bring to a boil, reduce the heat, and simmer until soft. Push the mixture through a non-metal strainer into a bowl. Chill.

4

Remove the ice cream from the freezer and let soften until spreadable. Spoon one-third of the mixture into a shallow square or rectangular container lined with plastic wrap. Mark parallel uneven furrows in the ice cream, then pipe the raspberry purée into the furrows. Carefully spread over another layer of softened ice cream, repeating until all the ice cream and raspberry mixture has been used. Finish with more wobbly stripes of ripple. Freeze until set.

5

To serve, remove from the container, discard the plastic wrap, and trim the sides straight if necessary. Serve alone or with fresh raspberries.

Rosewater-poached rhubarb
with vanilla ricotta

Rhubarb needs the briefest of cooking—especially if you want the stems to keep their shape. Forced rhubarb, around in spring, has the best pink color.

1 lb. rhubarb, cut into bite-sized chunks

¾ cup sugar

a squeeze of lemon juice

1½ tablespoons rosewater

3 cups ricotta cheese

1 vanilla bean, split lengthwise

1 tablespoon superfine sugar

3 tablespoons heavy cream

Serves 6

Variations:

• Serve the rhubarb with mascarpone beaten with ground almonds and vanilla sugar.

• Add a pinch of saffron threads or slivers of candied ginger to the rhubarb juice.

• Serve the vanilla ricotta with a pile of berries or bake into a cheesecake and top with the poached rhubarb.

1

To cook the rhubarb, put the sugar, lemon juice, and ½ cup water into a saucepan, stir, and bring to a boil. Turn down the heat and simmer gently until all the sugar has dissolved. Add the chunks of rhubarb and stir again to coat. Simmer for about 3 minutes. Gently turn over the rhubarb, cover the pan with a lid, turn off the heat, stir in the rosewater, and let cool.

2

Using a wooden spoon, press the ricotta through a sieve into a bowl. Scrape the seeds from the vanilla bean into the ricotta and mix well. Dissolve the sugar in the cream and beat into the ricotta. Chill.

3

Spoon the rhubarb and rosewater juices into bowls or onto small serving plates and serve with the vanilla ricotta in spoonfuls, or in a separate bowl.

Caramel syrup apples

with thick whipped cream

I love tarte Tatin—the soaked flaky pastry is good, but what makes it for me is the combination of melting apple saturated in caramel and all that extra buttery syrup that runs in rivulets into a pool of cream on the plate. So why not do just that? Forget about pastry, and have apples, buttery caramel, and loads of cream. A seriously sensuous windfall in a bowl.

6 medium apples

juice of 1 lemon

2½ cups sugar

½ cup butter

1 teaspoon ground cinnamon

1¼ cups heavy cream, whipped, or crème fraîche

Serves 6

1

Peel the apples and put into a bowl of water mixed with lemon juice to stop them turning brown.

2

Put the sugar into a small saucepan with 1 tablespoon water, and cook over a gentle heat until golden and turned to a light caramel. Stir in the butter.

3

Drain the apples, pack into a deep dish, sprinkle with cinnamon and pour over the toffee caramel. Cover loosely with foil and bake in a preheated oven at 350°F for 45 minutes or until the apples are very tender.

4

Serve in bowls with whipped cream or crème fraîche.

Blistered peaches with chile kaffir lime ice

Chile and kaffir lime ice is addictive. It may sound strange but it works. The sharp iciness of the lime kicks in first and the chile infusion adds a warming aftertaste. Particularly good with these caramelized peaches.

3 large peaches, halved and pitted

2 tablespoons dark brown sugar

1 teaspoon ground allspice

2 tablespoons butter, softened

Kaffir lime ice:

5 limes, preferably kaffir limes*
(grated zest of 2, juice of 5)

3 small hot chiles, split and seeded

2 cups confestioner's sugar, sifted

2 cups crème fraîche

3 tablespoons ice water

Serves 6

Note: Available at Asian specialty markets.

1

To make the ice, put the lime zest and juice, the chiles, and confectioner's sugar in a bowl and mix to dissolve the sugar. Set aside for 30 minutes to develop the flavors.

2

Remove and discard the chiles. Beat the crème fraîche thoroughly into the lime syrup. Spoon into a covered container and freeze—there is no need to stir. Remove from the freezer and leave at room temperature for 10 minutes before serving.

3

Just before serving, sprinkle the peach halves with sugar and allspice, then smear with butter. Lightly brown under a hot broiler. Put half a peach in each bowl and serve with the ice.

Variations:

• For a lighter ice, use whipped heavy cream instead of crème fraîche.

• Serve the ice with sautéed or broiled bananas, or stir through raspberry purée to make a ripple.

• Serve the peaches with crème fraîche beaten with ginger syrup or toasted pine nuts and yogurt.

151

Ginger toffee pears with rice pudding

Rice pudding isn't just nursery food—it's rib-sticking good, as my grandfather used to say. Sometimes, a bit of plain honest home cooking is just what we need, but with these toffee pears, it's good enough for a dinner party.

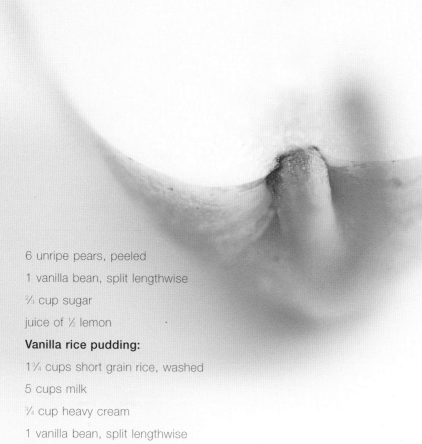

6 unripe pears, peeled

1 vanilla bean, split lengthwise

⅔ cup sugar

juice of ½ lemon

Vanilla rice pudding:

1¾ cups short grain rice, washed

5 cups milk

¾ cup heavy cream

1 vanilla bean, split lengthwise

¼ cup sugar

Ginger toffee:

2 inches fresh ginger, chopped

¾ cup sugar

3 tablespoons unsalted butter

Serves 6

1

To make the rice pudding, pour boiling water over the rice and soak for 3 minutes. Drain, put into a saucepan, add the milk, vanilla bean, and sugar, and simmer gently for 30 minutes. Discard the bean, stir in the cream, and spoon into a gratin dish. Cook in a preheated oven at 300°F for about 45 minutes.

2

To prepare the pears, put all the ingredients in a saucepan and cover with water. Simmer for 25–30 minutes or until tender. If not using immediately, let cool in the syrup. When ready to serve, remove from the syrup and heat through on top of the rice pudding.

3

To make the toffee, put the ginger, sugar, and 2 tablespoons water into a small saucepan and heat gently until the mixture becomes a good caramel color (watch it, as soon as it goes a deep red-amber color, it's close to burning). Stir in the butter, then add 5 tablespoons water, and stir well. Strain to remove the pieces of ginger. Pour some of the toffee over the pears, and serve the rest in a pitcher.

Lemongrass yogurt rice

with crushed raspberries

Mix and match the refreshing lemongrass yogurt rice with the sweet crushed fruit as you go—or you could even spoon the berries and juice into the bowls first and cover with the rice, then dig deep for the berries as you eat.

8 oz. raspberries

⅔ cup sugar

1 tablespoon lemon juice

½ cup short-grain rice, washed

4 stalks lemongrass, trimmed and smashed open

3 cups milk

1 lb. creamy yogurt

Serves 6

1

Put half the raspberries in a saucepan and stir in half the sugar and 1 tablespoon water. Bring to a boil, then reduce the heat, and simmer until the fruit is soft. Push the fruit and juice through a non-metal strainer into a bowl, discarding the pips. Stir in the lemon juice, then add the remaining raspberries to the purée, crush lightly, and let cool.

2

Put the rice, lemongrass, milk, and the remaining sugar into a saucepan, bring to a boil, stir well, reduce the heat, and simmer for 30 minutes. Let cool, then discard the lemongrass.

3

Stir the yogurt into the lemongrass rice, then divide between 6 bowls and serve with small bowls of crushed raspberries.

Variations:

• Flavor the rice with a split vanilla bean rather than lemongrass and serve with a purée of mixed berries.

• Serve the berries with thick yogurt and honey, sprinkled with toasted slivered almonds.

154

Summer pudding toast

Traditional English summer pudding, made from melted berries and juice-soaked bread, is delicious, but needs planning, to give it time to saturate and set. This combination of berry juices and strawberries on toast is an instant version—though the fruit mixture will still benefit from being left for a few hours if you have time. It looks just as elegant as the original.

4 baskets mixed berries, such as redcurrants, raspberries, blueberries, and blackberries, about 1 lb.

6 tablespoons sugar

½ lb. strawberries, stems removed and halved

6 slices brioche or white bread

To serve:

wild strawberries (optional)

mint leaves

confectioner's sugar, for dusting

thickened heavy cream

Serves 6

1
Pick over the baskets of fruit, removing any stems or leaves. Put the berries in a saucepan with ¼ cup water and the sugar. Bring to a boil, then reduce the heat, and simmer gently for about 8 minutes.

2
Put the halved strawberries in a bowl and press the cooked fruit syrup through a non-metal strainer over the strawberries. Let stand for at least 30 minutes, then chill. Alternatively, leave overnight in the refrigerator.

3
When ready to serve, toast the brioche or bread and spoon the fruit syrup over each slice. Arrange the glazed strawberries over the tops, surround with wild strawberries, if using, and sugar-dusted mint leaves. Serve the cream in a separate bowl or jug.

Variations:

• You needn't strain the fruit, just pile it all on toast, top with thick cream and serve.

• Try using warmed doughnuts instead of toast.

• Serve the berry juice and strawberry mixture with vanilla ice cream.

Peach and fig almond tart

A fail-safe pudding, that's straight forward to make—and doesn't involve rolling out pastry. The fruit just gets on with the work as it bakes, creating a wonderful soft almond and blistered fruit filling, oozing nectarlike juice.

8 sheets phyllo pastry, or enough to make 4 layers

melted butter, for greasing and brushing

1 tablespoon sugar

1 egg, lightly beaten

½ lb. mascarpone

4 tablespoons ground almonds

4 ripe peaches, pitted and sliced

4 figs, halved or quartered

1 tablespoon dark brown sugar, preferably unrefined

Serves 6

Variations:

• Substitute other fruits, such as blueberries and plums, nectarines, or poached pears.

1

Grease a 14 x 4 inch rectangular or 8½ inch circular pie pan and line with a single layer of phyllo pastry (about 2 overlapping sheets). Trim the pastry leaving about ½ inch sticking up above the rim of the pan. Brush with melted butter and line with another 2 sheets of pastry. Repeat until all the pastry has been used.

2

Beat the sugar and egg in a bowl, then beat in the mascarpone and almonds. Spread over the base of the tart.

3

Arrange the pieces of peaches and figs all over the mascarpone cream until the pie shell is full. Sprinkle with the brown sugar and brush more butter over the pastry and fruit.

4

Put on a baking tray and bake on the middle shelf of a preheated oven at 400°F for about 35 minutes or until tinged golden brown.

Rhubarb and custard pastries

Rhubarb and custard is a favorite combination, but put them on a pastry with a sprinkling of almonds and you have something downright fabulous. You can cheat a little if you like and buy ready-made custard, but making your own is so easy it's worth trying.

5 stalks young rhubarb, cut into 2-inch lengths

2 tablespoons sugar

1 vanilla bean, split lengthwise

1¼ cups milk

⅔ cup heavy cream

4 large egg yolks

6 tablespoons superfine sugar

2 tablespoons all-purpose flour

1 package frozen puff pastry (1 lb.), thawed

1 tablespoon chopped blanched almonds

confectioner's sugar, for dusting

Serves 6

1

Spread the rhubarb across a wide saucepan in a single layer, sprinkle with the sugar, and add about 3 tablespoons water. Heat to simmering, carefully turn over the slices, turn off the heat, and cover with a lid—the rhubarb should be poached through and tender. Let cool.

2

Put the split vanilla bean, milk, and cream in a saucepan and bring to a boil. Remove from the heat.

3

Beat 3 of the egg yolks, sugar, and flour in a bowl until thick and pale. Slowly beat in the hot vanilla milk (discard the bean). Pour the custard back into the milk pan and cook very gently, stirring all the time, for about 1 minute—don't let it boil, or it will curdle. Remove from the heat.

4

Roll out the puff pastry to ¼ inch thick and cut into small square shapes or a long rectangle. Spread custard over the top, leaving a ¼-inch edge of pastry uncovered. Top with lines of rhubarb, push the nuts into the pastry, and brush with the remaining egg yolk, beaten. Dust with confectioner's sugar and bake in a preheated oven at 400°F for 20 minutes for small pastries or 30 minutes if large—or until puffed and golden.

5

Dust with more confectioner's sugar and serve warm.

Pear tart with Catalan custard

A line of pears put to bed on a puffed blanket of pastry. I've used a thin, *crème-anglaise*-style custard flavored with citrus peel, as the Spanish do to make *crème catalan*. It can be thickened with 2 teaspoons of cornstarch.

1 tablespoon lemon juice

4 unripe pears

1 vanilla bean, split lengthwise

⅔ cup sugar

1 lb. fresh, ready-made puff pastry

1 egg, lightly beaten

confectioner's sugar, for dusting

Catalan custard:

1¼ cups milk

1¼ cups heavy cream

2 cinnamon sticks, broken

grated zest of ½ lemon

½ cup sugar

6 egg yolks

Serves 8

1

Put the milk, cream, cinnamon, and lemon in a saucepan and bring to a boil. Remove from the heat and set aside for 30 minutes.

2

Half fill a saucepan with water and add the lemon juice. Peel the pears and put them straight into the pan to stop browning. Add the vanilla bean and sugar, bring to a boil, and simmer for 25 minutes until just tender.

3

Roll out the pastry, ⅛–¼ inch thick, and cut into 2 long strips, each big enough to fit 4 pear halves, side by side with about ½ inch between. Put on a greased baking tray. Arrange the halved pears across the dough and, with the tip of a knife, score a shallow cut in the dough around each pear. Brush all over with beaten egg. Bake in a preheated oven at 400°F for 20–30 minutes until puffed and golden.

4

Beat the sugar and egg yolks together in a bowl. Strain the milk mixture and beat into the egg mixture. Pour into a saucepan and heat gently, continuously stirring, until you have a thin custard that coats the back of the spoon (too much heat and the custard will curdle).

5

Dust the tart with confectioner's sugar, cut in wedges, and serve with custard.

Baby apple pies

Pure unadulterated apple. No fancy flavors or hidden extras—apples can make it on their own. Cooked until silky smooth with a few little chunks for texture, then baked inside a buttery crumbly pastry, this is real comfort food.

2½ cups all-purpose flour

1 cup sugar, plus extra for dusting

¾ cup butter, softened

3 medium egg yolks

mascarpone cheese, to serve

Apple filling:

4 large baking apples,
peeled, cored, and chopped

¼ cup sugar

juice of ½ lemon

Makes about 12

one 12-hole muffin tray

1

Put the flour in a large bowl, make a well in the center, and add the sugar. Add the butter and egg yolks. Using a fork, mash the yolks, butter, and sugar together, then draw in the flour. Using your hands, mix well, then transfer to a work surface, and knead well for about 30 seconds to form a smooth dough (add a little extra flour if necessary, to form the right consistency). Wrap in plastic and chill for 20 minutes.

2

Put the chopped apple in a saucepan with the sugar, lemon juice, and 2 tablespoons water and cook to a coarse purée, leaving a few lumps. Taste and add more sugar if you prefer. Cool, then chill.

3

Roll out the pastry to ⅛ inch thick. Using a cookie cutter, stamp out 12 circles big enough to line the holes in a 12-hole mini muffin tray. Cut 12 smaller circles for lids. Line the molds with the larger circles of dough and fill with the apple mixture. Brush the rim of the dough with water, top with the smaller circles of dough, and gently press the edges together. Trim with a knife to make neat edges. Make 3 small neat holes in the top of each pie and dust with sugar.

4

Bake in a preheated oven 375°F for 20–25 minutes until golden at the edges. Cool a little, then remove, dust with more sugar, and serve with mascarpone.

Blueberry cheesecake

Yes, there's a pastry to make, but it's so easy, and rolling it straight onto the pan stops it tearing. Easy to make and light to eat, the filling is virtually fat free and the pastry base is so thin you can have seconds without worrying about calories. The base and filling hold up well if you want to make it in advance—add the fresh fruit just before serving.

10 oz. blueberries

mint leaves

confectioner's, for dusting

heavy cream, to serve (optional)

Pastry base:

5 tablespoons sugar

½ cup unsalted butter, softened

1 egg yolk

1 teaspoon grated lemon zest

1¼ cups all-purpose flour, sifted

Cheesecake filling:

1⅔ cup low-fat soft cheese

4 eggs, yolks and whites separated

1 teaspoon grated lemon zest

⅔ cup sugar

1 tablespoon all-purpose flour

166   *Serves 6–8*

1

Butter an 8-inch springform pan and base-line with waxed paper.

2

To prepare the pastry base, mix the sugar, butter, egg yolk, and lemon zest in a bowl. Add the flour and work to a smooth dough. If it is too sticky, dust with flour, then work in. Chill for 20 minutes.

3

Put the base of the springform tin on the work surface and roll out the pastry on top to approximately ⅛-inch thickness. Trim around the base with a knife and discard the excess dough. Assemble the pan and bake in a preheated oven at 300°F for 20 minutes until half cooked. Let cool. Reduce the oven heat to 275°F.

4

To make the cheesecake filling, mix the cheese in a bowl with the egg yolks and lemon zest. Beat the egg whites until stiff, then gradually beat in the sugar and flour. Fold the egg white mixture into the cheese mixture and spoon over the part-cooked pie shell in the pan. Sprinkle with 2 tablespoons of the berries and bake on the middle shelf of the oven for about 1 hour or until firm to the touch. Let cool.

5

To serve, top with a pile of the remaining fruit, sprinkle with a few mint leaves, dust with confectioner's sugar, and serve with cream, if using.

Passion cake

You wouldn't look twice at a passionfruit—that's if you didn't know what lay within. It looks far from passionate. The flower is extremely distinctive and this gives rise to its name, symbolizing the Passion of Christ. But the plainest of fruits contains within its hallowed skin a richly perfumed nectarlike mass of juices and seeds (which are edible too). Truly humble on the outside and full of divine things within—halve, scoop out the contents, and enjoy.

1¼ cups ground almonds

6½ tablespoons all-purpose flour, sifted

a pinch of salt

4 eggs, separated

1 vanilla bean, split lengthwise

¾ cup sugar

strained flesh and juice of 6 passionfruit

2 tablespoons confectioner's sugar

Passionfruit syrup:

flesh and seeds of 8 passionfruit

juice of ½ lemon

½ cup sugar

thick heavy cream or crème fraîche, to serve

Makes 8 individual heart-shaped cakes

eight 4-inch heart-shaped cake pans, greased and base-lined

1

Mix the ground almonds in a bowl with the flour and salt, and make a well in the center. In a second bowl, beat the egg yolks and sugar until the mixture is pale and leaves a trail when lifted. Scrape the seeds from the vanilla bean into the mixture, and beat well. Stir into the almond mixture, followed by the passionfruit juice.

2

Beat the egg whites to soft peak stage and fold into the cake mixture. Divide between 8 greased and base-lined 4-inch heart-shaped pans and bake in a preheated oven at 350°F for about 15–20 minutes until the cake springs back when lightly pressed. Turn out onto a wire rack. Let cool.

3

Put all the syrup ingredients into a small saucepan and heat to make a thin syrup. Lightly dust the cakes with confectioner's sugar and serve in a pool of syrup with heavy cream or créme fraîche.

Variation:

• Make a large cake, cool, and slice into 3 layers. Fill each layer with mascarpone flavored with lemon curd.

Hazelnut tiramisu cake

For an alternative topping, melt 8 oz. bitter chocolate with ½ cup heavy cream and let cool. Beat until thick, then spread the mixture over the top and sides of the cake, swirling it into a pattern and decorate with toasted hazelnuts.

4 eggs

1¼ cups sugar

1¼ cups flour, sifted

⅔ cup hazelnuts, roasted, skinned, and coarsely ground

1 teaspoon vanilla extract

Tiramisu filling:

2 eggs

2 tablespoons sugar

1½ lb. mascarpone

1 cup heavy cream

½ cup strong coffee (cold)

4 tablespoons coffee liqueur, such as Kahlúa

unsweetened cocoa powder, for dusting (optional)

Chocolate band (optional):*

11 oz. bitter chocolate, broken into pieces

Serves 4–6

2 round 7-inch springform cake pans, buttered and base-lined with parchment paper.

1

To make the cake, beat the eggs with an electric beater or mixer until frothy. Gradually beat in the sugar until the mixture is absolutely white and holds its shape. Fold in the flour, hazelnuts, and vanilla. Divide the mixture between the prepared cake pans. Bake in a preheated oven at 350ºF for 25–30 minutes, or until firm to the touch. Let cool, then remove the paper and slice each sponge into 2 rounds.

2

To make the filling, beat the eggs with the sugar in a large bowl, then beat in the mascarpone. Reserve one-third of the mixture in a small bowl. Beat the cream to soft peak stage and fold into the mixture in the large bowl. Mix the coffee with the coffee liqueur in a cup or small pitcher.

3

To assemble the cake, put a round of sponge on a serving plate and sprinkle with the liqueur coffee mixture. Cover with a thick layer of mascarpone cream. Top with another round of sponge and repeat the process until all the sponge has been used. (Don't sprinkle coffee right to the edges and leave the top sponge unsprinkled.) Using a spatula, cover the top and sides of the cake with the reserved mascarpone. Add the chocolate band (see note). Chill. Dust with cocoa powder if you like.

*Note: To make the Chocolate Band, melt the chocolate in a heatproof bowl set over a pan of simmering water until smooth and lump-free. Cut out a rectangle of thick plastic measuring the circumference x height of the assembled cake. Set on a smooth work surface. Pour the mixture over the plastic, spreading with a spatula until the edges are covered. Smooth level. Let cool until almost set, but still pliable. Lift up the plastic band and bend it around the cake (chocolate on the inside) with a small overlapping "seam" and secure with tape. Chill until set, then remove the tape, and peel off the plastic.

Caramel nut shortbread

Caramel squares, often found in old-fashioned bakeries, cafés, and English tea shops, are deliciously decadent. Sweetly addictive, they will work wonders (in the wrong direction) to your waistline. Eat one, do 80 push-ups, that's the way to do it. I make mine with nuts and raisins.

2 cups all-purpose flour

a pinch of salt

½ cup plus 2 tablespoons sugar

1 cup unsalted butter

1¼ cups plump raisins

2¼ cups pecans or walnut halves

7 oz. bitter chocolate

Caramel:

½ cup unsalted butter

½ cup plus 2 tablespoons light brown sugar

2 tablespoons light corn syrup

6 oz. sweetened condensed milk (1 small can)

Serves 4–6

12- x 8- inch jelly roll pan

1

To make the shortbread, put the flour, salt, sugar, and butter into a food processor and pulse until the dough forms a ball. Alternatively, using your fingertips, rub the butter into the flour until the mixture resembles fine crumbs, then work in the salt and sugar. Press the mixture into the jelly roll pan. Sprinkle with raisins and press flat. Bake in a preheated oven at 350°F for 25–30 minutes or until golden.

2

Put all the caramel ingredients into a nonstick saucepan and heat gently, but do not boil. Beat thoroughly together.

3

Line the nuts across the cooked shortbread base, then pour over the hot caramel mixture. Smooth with a spatula and chill until firm.

4

Melt the chocolate in a heatproof bowl set over a saucepan of gently simmering water. Pour the chocolate over the set caramel mixture, smooth with a spatula, and let set. Cut into bars or fingers before serving.

index

A

allspice cabbage with shallots and sausages, 140

almonds: peach and fig almond tart, 159

Persian chicken with coconut and almonds, 102

anchovy baked toast, Caesar greens with, 36

anise braised pork with Chinese mustard cabbage, 135

apples: baby apple pies, 165

caramel syrup apples, 148

pecan pork with apple and maple syrup, 137

pot-roasted game bird with apple, cabbage, juniper, and cream, 116

Asian greens, asparagus soup with, 11

asparagus: asparagus brunch with prosciutto toasts, 22

asparagus phyllo tart with spinach and potato, 45

asparagus soup with Asian greens, 11

salmon fish fingers with asparagus, spring pods, and mustard-mint butter, 88

avocado and cilantro toast, 28

B

baba ganoush, 127

bacon: bacon-wrapped monkfish with Brussels tops, 85

pea quiche, 32

basil oil, spinach gnocchi with, 50

beans: roasted vine tomatoes with cannellini bean salad, 38

beef: beef stew with chestnuts, 122

pub beef and onion pies, 124

beer batter, fish fillets in, 87

bhajia, corn and sweet potato, 55

blackened salmon with oven-roasted tomato salad, 80

blistered peaches with chile kaffir lime ice, 151

blueberry cheesecake, 166

bread: Caesar greens with anchovy baked toast, 36

honeyed duck with baby chard, cilantro, and mustard seed mayo in ciabatta, 108

roasted tomatoes in herb oil with char-grilled bread, 24–5

Brussels sprouts, Christmas turkey for two with clove stuffing and. 115

Brussels tops, bacon-wrapped monkfish with, 85

butternut squash: grilled chicken and pumpkin couscous, 98

C

caramel nut shortbread, 172

cabbage: allspice cabbage with shallots and sausages, 140

pot-roasted game bird with apple, cabbage, juniper, and cream, 116

Caesar greens with anchovy baked toast, 36

cakes: hazelnut tiramisu cake, 171

passion cake, 168

cannellini bean salad, roasted vine tomatoes with, 38

caramel syrup apples, 148

Catalan custard, pear tart with, 162

celery root: pastrami salmon with caraway celery root, 78

chard: honeyed duck with baby chard, cilantro and mustard seed mayo in ciabatta, 108

cheese: eggplant mozzarella lasagne, 48

Indian coconut dhaal with peas and paneer, 52

porcini pizza with garlic butter, 67

pot-roasted red onions with feta cheese and oregano, 62

roasted mushrooms with horseradish mascarpone, 30

roasted tomatoes in herb oil with baby mozzarella, 24–5

rosewater-poached rhubarb with vanilla ricotta, 146

spinach gnocchi with basil oil, 50

summer pasta, 46

cheesecake, blueberry, 166

chestnuts, beef stew with, 122

chicken, 92–106

char-grilled chicken and pumpkin couscous, 98

chicken and butter leek soup, 13

chicken and mushroom pie, 106

chicken and pea shoot salad, 95

mango lapsang chicken and herb salad, 97

Persian chicken with coconut and almonds, 102

prosciutto chicken kiev with peas, fava beans, mint, and basil, 101

chickpeas: fava bean falafels, 41

cilantro: avocado and cilantro toast, 28

chiles: chile crisp shrimp and garlic chives, 71

chile kaffir lime ice, 151

kumquat duck with chile citrus sauce, 110

sambal dips, 55

Chinese mustard cabbage, anise braised pork with, 135

chocolate: hazelnut tiramisu cake, 171

caramel nut shortbread, 172

chowder, Jerusalem artichoke, 18

Christmas turkey for two, 115

clay pot lemon poussin, 104

coconut milk: Indian coconut dhaal, 52

Persian chicken with coconut and almonds, 102

pumpkin coconut curry, 59

coffee: hazelnut tiramisu cake, 171

corn cobs: corn and sweet potato bhajia with sambal dip, 55

seafood and corn gumbo, 73

couscous: char-grilled chicken and pumpkin couscous, 98

curries: green tomato and basil curry, 56

pumpkin coconut curry, 59

shrimp and aubergine laksa, 75

custard: pear tart with Catalan custard, 162

rhubarb and custard pastries, 160

D

desserts, 142–72

duck: honeyed duck with baby chard, cilantro and mustard seed mayo in ciabatta, 108

kumquat duck with chile citrus sauce, 110

root and honey duck hot pot, 113

E

eggs: asparagus brunch with prosciutto soldiers, 22

Indian spiced aubergine with egg, basil and cardamom rice, 60–1

eggplants: eggplant croutons, 16

baba ganoush, 127

eggplant mozzarella lasagne, 48

Indian spiced eggplant, 60–1

lamb burgers with char-grilled eggplant, hummus, seed salt, and mint, 127

shrimp and eggplant laksa, 75

F

fava beans: fava bean falafels, 41

prosciutto chicken kiev with peas and, 101

falafels, fava bean, 41

figs: peach and fig almond tart, 159

fish and seafood, 68–91

fish fillets in beer batter, 87

fish fingers, salmon, 88

fishcakes: smoked fishcakes with lemon butter spinach, 90

fruit: green fruit gado gado with lime and peanut dressing, 26

summer pudding toast, 157

G

gado gado, green fruit, 26

game bird, pot-roasted, 116

garlic: porcini pizza with garlic butter, 67

rosemary and olive lamb with roasted garlic lima beans, 128

garlic chives, chile crisp shrimp and, 71

ginger toffee pears with rice pudding, 152

gnocchi: spinach gnocchi with basil oil, 50

goat cheese, pumpkin soup with Creole roasted pumpkin seeds and, 14

green fruit gado gado, 26

green tomato and basil curry, 56

greens: Caesar greens with anchovy baked toast, 36

pot-roasted game bird with apple, cabbage, juniper, and cream, 116

H

ham and peas, 139

hazelnut tiramisu cake, 171

honeyed duck, 108

horseradish picada, bacon-wrapped monkfish with, 85

roasted mushrooms with horseradish mascarpone, 30

thyme buttered baby roots with homemade horseradish cream, 64

hot water crust pastry, 124

I

ice cream: chile kaffir lime ice, 151

raspberry ripple, 144

Indian coconut dhaal, 52

Indian spiced eggplant, 60–1

J

Jerusalem artichoke chowder with pan-seared scallops, 18

K

kaffir limes: chile kaffir lime ice, 151

kumquat duck with chile citrus sauce, 110

L

lamb: lamb burgers with char-grilled eggplant, 127

lamb shanks with squash ratatouille, 130

rosemary and olive lamb, 128

lasagne: eggplant mozzarella lasagne, 48

summer pasta, 46

leeks: chicken and butter leek soup, 13

lemon: clay pot lemon poussin, 104

lemon herb-cured salmon trout, 76

lemongrass yogurt rice, 154

lima beans: rosemary and olive lamb with roasted garlic lima beans, 128

limes: chile kaffir lime ice, 151

M

mango lapsang chicken and herb salad, 97

meat, 120–41

monkfish, bacon-wrapped, 85

morels: chicken and mushroom pie, 106

mushrooms: chicken and mushroom pie, 106

porcini pizza with garlic butter, 67

pork chops with peppered wild mushroom gravy, 132

roasted mushrooms with horseradish mascarpone, 30

N

noodles: prawn and eggplant laksa, 75
    spice island noodle soup, 20

O

okra: seafood and corn gumbo, 73
olives: lamb shanks with ratatouille, 130
    rosemary and olive lamb, 128
onions: pot-roasted red onions, 62
    pub beef and onion pies, 124
oranges: kumquat duck with chile citrus sauce, 110

P

paneer, Indian coconut dhaal with peas and, 52
passion cake, 168
pastrami salmon with caraway celeriac, 78
pastries, rhubarb and custard, 160
pastry, hot water crust, 124
pea shoots: chicken and pea shoot salad, 95
peaches: blistered peaches with chilei kaffir lime ice, 151
    peach and fig almond tart, 159
    squab and peach tagine, 119
peanuts: green fruit gado gado with lime and peanut dressing, 26
pears: ginger toffee pears, 152
    pear tart with Catalan custard, 162
peas: fish fillets in beer batter with pea purée, 87
    ham and peas, 139
    Indian coconut dhaal with paneer and, 52
    pea quiche, 32
    prosciutto chicken kiev with, 101
peas, yellow split: Indian coconut dhaal, 52
pecan nuts: caramel nut shortbread, 172
    pecan pork with apple and maple syrup, 137
peppers: lamb shanks with squash ratatouille, 130
    tomato and pepper soup, 16
Persian chicken with coconut and almonds, 102
pies: baby apple pies, 165
    chicken and mushroom pie, 106
    pub beef and onion pies, 124
pigeon: squab and peach tagine, 119
pizzas: porcini pizza with garlic butter, 67
porcini pizza with garlic butter, 67
pork: anise braised pork with Chinese mustard cabbage, 135
    pecan pork with apple and maple syrup, 137
    pork chops with peppered wild mushroom gravy, 132

spice island noodle soup, 20
potatoes: asparagus phyllo tart with spinach and, 45
    lemon herb-cured salmon trout with dill potatoes, 76
    smoked fishcakes, 90
poussin, clay pot lemon, 104
    shrimp and eggplant laksa, 75
    spice island noodle soup, 20
prosciutto chicken kiev, 101
prosciutto soldiers, asparagus brunch with, 22
pub beef and onion pies, 124
pumpkin: char-grilled chicken and pumpkin couscous, 98
    pumpkin coconut curry, 59
    pumpkin soup with Creole roasted pumpkin seeds, 14

Q

quiche, pea, 32

R

raisins: caramel shortbread, 172
raspberries: lemongrass yogurt rice with crushed raspberries, 154
    raspberry ripple, 144
ratatouille: lamb shanks with squash ratatouille, 130
rhubarb: rhubarb and custard pastries, 160
    rosewater-poached rhubarb with vanilla ricotta, 146
rice: ginger toffee pears with rice pudding, 152
    Indian spiced eggplant with egg, basil, and cardamom rice, 60-1
    lemongrass yogurt rice, 154
root vegetables: root and honey duck hot pot, 113
    thyme buttered baby roots, 64
rosemary and olive lamb, 128
rosewater-poached rhubarb, 146

S

salads: blackened salmon with oven-roasted tomato salad, 80
    chicken and pea shoot salad, 95
    dill potato salad, 76
    green fruit gado gado, 26
    herb radish salad, 41
    mango lapsang chicken and herb salad, 97
    roasted vine tomatoes with cannellini bean salad, 38
salmon: blackened salmon, 80
    fish fillets in beer batter, 87
    pastrami salmon with caraway celery root, 78
    salmon fish fingers, 88
salmon trout, lemon herb-cured, 76
sausages, allspice cabbage with shallots and, 140

scallops: Jerusalem artichoke chowder with pan-seared scallops, 18
sea bass: steamed sea bass with snowpeas and soy beans, 82
seafood, 68–91
seafood and corn gumbo, 73
shortbread, caramel nut, 172
shrimp: chile crisp shrimp and garlic chives, 71
snowpeas: steamed sea bass with soy beans and, 82
smoked fishcakes with lemon butter spinach, 90
smoking chicken, 97
soups, 8–20
    asparagus soup with Asian greens, 11
    chicken and butter leek soup, 13
    Jerusalem artichoke chowder, 18
    pumpkin soup with Creole roasted pumpkin seeds, 14
    spice island noodle soup, 20
    tomato and pepper soup, 16
soy beans, steamed sea bass with snowpeas and, 82
spaghetti squash: pumpkin coconut curry, 59
spice island noodle soup, 20
spinach: asparagus phyllo tart with potato and, 45
    smoked fishcakes with lemon butter spinach, 90
    spinach gnocchi with basil oil, 50
squab and peach tagine, 119
squash: char-grilled chicken and pumpkin couscous, 98
    lamb shanks with squash ratatouille, 130
summer pasta, 46
summer pudding toast, 157
sweet potatoes: corn and sweet potato bhajia, 55

T

tagine, squab and peach, 119
tarts: asparagus phyllo tart, 45
    peach and fig almond tart, 159
    pear tart with Catalan custard, 162
    tomato and bell pepper tart, 42
thyme buttered baby roots, 64
tiramisu cake, hazelnut, 171
toast: avocado and cilantro toast, 28
    Caesar greens with anchovy baked toast, 36
    roasted mushrooms with horseradish mascarpone, 30
    summer pudding toast, 157
toffee: ginger toffee pears, 152
tomatoes: blackened salmon with

oven-roasted tomato salad, 80
    green tomato and basil curry, 56
    roasted tomatoes in herb oil, 24-5
    roasted vine tomatoes with cannellini bean salad, 38
    sambal dips, 55
    summer pasta, 46
    tomato and pepper soup, 16
    tomato and bell pepper tart, 42
turkey: Christmas turkey for two, 115

V

vegetables, 34–67
    root and honey duck hot pot, 113
    thyme buttered baby roots, 64

W

water spinach: asparagus soup with Asian greens, 11

Y

yogurt: lemongrass yogurt rice, 154

Z

zucchini: summer pasta, 46

Acknowledgments

My thanks to Egg, of Kinnerton Street, Belgravia, London, who were so generous in lending beautiful bowls for photography, and Kara Kara, of Tokyo and Pond Place, South Kensington in London, for Japanese ceramics and other props; to the Conran Shop, Fulham Road, London, for the white ceramic platters. Thanks also to City Herbs of New Spitalfield Market, London and Panzas, 19 Circus Road, London NW8 for great fruit and vegetables. Finally, many thanks to Halcyon Herbs for the salad leaves and herbs. They sell seeds by mail order from 10 Hampden Close, Chalgrove, Oxford, OX44 7SB, England. Fax 01865 890 180.